STUDENT'S BOOK 1

RICHARD HARRISON

NEW
ENGLISH PLEASE

eBOOK

ALWAYS LEARNING

PEARSON

Contents

Wordlist p.108

Functions	Pronunciation	
greeting people (formally and informally) introducing self and others	rising and falling intonation word and sentence stress letters of the alphabet – sound groups	
introducing/talking about members of the family. asking about/explaining city/country of origin	sounds	/ð/ this /θ/ thanks /p/ push /b/ brother
introductions (2 or more people) asking about: job, nationality, country, offering something to someone (informally) describing/asking about feelings	vowels diphthongs	/i/ these /ɪ/ this /ɪə/ we're /eə/ they're
identifying places describing buildings, objects asking directions describing location buying and selling products	diphthongs consonants intonation of questions	/eə/ there /ɪə/ here /oʊ/ those /ʃ/ English /tʃ/ watch
describing objects describing people asking for descriptions telling the time talking about possessions	who silent letter r vowels	
asking for/giving directions describing location describing rooms asking to speak to someone requesting/offering help	sounds silent letters p, r	/e/ left /ɪ/ lift /ɜ:/ third /eə/ there /ɔ:/ door

0 Check up!

Classroom language and numbers لغة الفصل وأرقام

Look.	اُنظر
Say.	قل
Write.	اُكتب
Listen.	اِسمع
Read.	اِقرأ
Match.	ماثل (ضاهٍ)
Ask.	اِسأل
Answer.	أجب
Numbers	الأعداد

1 Look ۱ اُنظر

0   1   2   3   4   5   6   7   8   9   10

2 Match ۲ ماثل

3 Listen and repeat ۳ اِسمع و كرر

0   1   2   3   4   5   6   7   8   9   10

4 🔊 **Listen and circle**   اسمع و ارسم ٤

1	0	1	2	3	4	⑤	6	7	8	9	10
2	0	1	2	3	4	5	6	7	8	9	10
3	0	1	2	3	4	5	6	7	8	9	10
4	0	1	2	3	4	5	6	7	8	9	10
5	0	1	2	3	4	5	6	7	8	9	10
6	0	1	2	3	4	5	6	7	8	9	10
7	0	1	2	3	4	5	6	7	8	9	10
8	0	1	2	3	4	5	6	7	8	9	10
9	0	1	2	3	4	5	6	7	8	9	10
10	0	1	2	3	4	5	6	7	8	9	10
11	0	1	2	3	4	5	6	7	8	9	10

5 **Write**   اُكتب ٥

Copy the numbers.   اِنسخ الأرقام

. ٠   0 0 0

١   1 1 1

٢   2 2 2

٣   3 3 3

٤   4 4 4

٥   5 5 5

٦   6 6 6

٧   7 7 7

٨   8 8 8

٩   9 9 9

6 **Write** اُكتب ٦

Write the numbers.

3

7 🔊 **Listen and write** اِسمع واكتب ٧

Telephone numbers أرقام التلفونات

7 _____

3 _____

8 _____

4 _____

3 _____

0 _____

The Alphabet – capital letters   حروف الهجاء – الحروف الكبيرة

A B C D E F G H I J K L M N O P Q R S T U V W X Y Z

1 🔊 **Listen and repeat**   ١ إسمع وكرر

A H J K	B C D E G P T V

F L M N S X Z	I Y	O

Q U W	R

2 **Read and match**   ٢ إقرأ وماثل

A	Ⓐ	C	D	H	E	F	T	Ⓐ	U	X	R	Ⓐ
B	G	K	P	S	N	O	B	D	P	B	W	D
C	O	U	V	C	B	G	Q	C	T	U	C	G
D	B	D	E	Q	U	P	B	D	P	X	S	R
E	F	H	L	E	C	V	K	L	F	H	B	E
F	K	L	E	R	G	H	F	P	F	R	F	B
G	C	B	G	R	O	G	Q	C	G	H	Q	G
H	A	T	F	K	M	H	T	D	W	H	X	A
i	L	F	I	T	A	V	L	I	T	I	F	J
J	K	I	F	T	S	J	L	P	I	T	J	M
K	F	J	L	R	P	T	K	X	H	R	K	K
L	T	L	F	I	J	T	L	Z	V	T	L	N
M	N	V	M	L	W	M	V	N	M	W	D	H
N	B	G	I	N	W	P	Q	L	T	A	N	J
O	O	D	C	G	Q	O	D	Q	C	O	U	C
P	R	P	B	D	R	B	C	T	P	R	B	S
Q	U	G	Q	C	O	S	Q	G	O	Q	E	B
R	B	R	P	R	D	J	P	Y	R	S	P	B
S	F	B	H	M	Z	S	U	B	Z	G	S	H
T	H	F	E	L	I	F	T	B	T	E	I	T
U	V	U	Y	V	U	O	W	U	V	U	A	
V	A	L	D	V	T	U	W	S	U	V	P	Q
W	U	H	X	K	W	W	B	V	L	W	U	A
X	X	H	D	S	V	X	V	K	E	X	Y	
Y	V	K	Y	S	T	Y	W	I	V	I	V	X
Z	E	F	Z	X	F	S	T	K	V	A	Z	S

3 Read and say   ٣ اِقرأ وقل

Read the abbreviations and match them with the pictures.   اِقرأ الاختصارات وضاهها مع الصور

1 FM

2 BMW

3 TV

4 OK   _SOS_   _____   _____

5 UK

6 USA

7 SOS

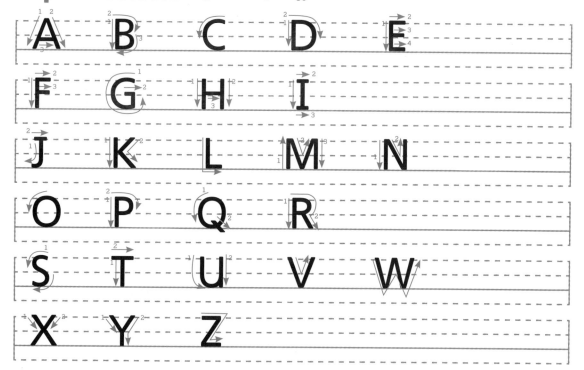

8 KLM   _____   _____   _____

Capital Letters   حروف الهجاء الكبيرة

A B C D E

F G H I

J K L M N

O P Q R

S T U V W

X Y Z

4 Write   أُكتب ٤

Copy the letters A – E.   اِنسخ الحروف

A ---

B ---

C ---

D ---

E ---

● Now listen and write.   والان اسمع واكتب

----

5 Write   أُكتب ٥

Copy the letters F – J.   اِنسخ الحروف

F ---

G ---

H ---

I ---

J ---

⊙ Now listen and write.   والآن اسمع واكتب

6 Write   ٦ أُكتب

Copy the letters K – O.   إِنسخ الحروف

K

L

M

N

O

⊙ Now listen and write.   والآن اسمع واكتب

7 Write   أُكتب ٧

Copy the letters P – T.   اِنسخ الحروف

P

Q

R

S

T

● Now listen and write.   والآن اسمع واكتب

8 Write   أُكتب ٨

Copy the letters U – Z.   اِنسخ الحروف

U

V

W

X

Y

Z

● Now listen and write.   والآن اسمع واكتب

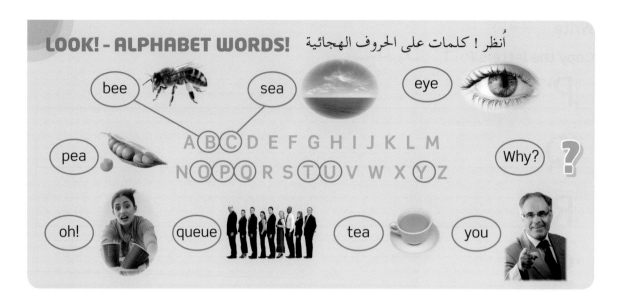

LOOK! - ALPHABET WORDS! أُنظر ! كلمات على الحروف الهجائية

bee

sea

eye

pea

A B C D E F G H I J K L M
N O P Q R S T U V W X Y Z

Why?

?

oh!

queue

tea

you

9 🔘 **Listen** اِسمع ٩

Passport numbers أرقام جواز السفر

1   2   3   4

_____   _____   _____   _____

Car numbers أرقام السيارات

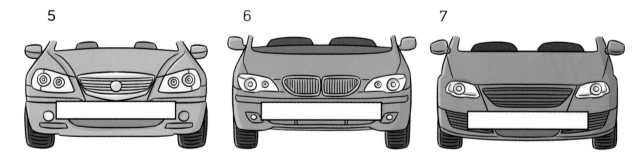

5   6   7

Flight numbers أرقام الرحلات الجوية

8	Cairo	_____
9	London	_____
10	Tunis	_____
11	Abu Dhabi	_____
12	Jeddah	_____
13	Damascus	_____

The Alphabet – Small letters الحروف الهجائية ـ الحروف الصغيرة

a b c d e f g h i j k l m n o p q r s t u v w x y z

1 Match ماثل ١

M R B T D U E A X
W L I Z N Q C S K
G O P J Y F V H

a b o z k f v q
s m p x j h r g
y c t i n e u w l d

2 Match ماثل ٢

a	a	c	e	o	e	u	v	e	a	s	c	o	a	e	x
b	p	d	f	k	b	l	d	p	d	b	l	k	t	b	d
c	e	o	d	c	e	q	o	u	v	c	d	o	a	g	c
d	d	b	t	y	k	t	d	b	d	t	p	b	d	f
e	o	a	c	s	u	r	e	v	d	e	a	o	e	s	g
f	t	s	g	f	h	k	t	s	b	l	f	g	t	k	d
g	g	p	q	h	g	j	y	q	p	d	g	q	d	p	j
h	m	k	f	t	n	b	h	k	t	f	h	d	l	h	n
i	i	l	j	t	v	i	y	l	j	t	j	i	y	f	l
j	y	l	g	l	q	p	j	l	i	j	y	q	f	p	i
k	h	f	b	k	h	x	t	j	c	f	d	x	v	h	t
l	t	f	i	k	f	l	t	f	b	i	l	d	j	t	h
m	m	u	w	n	v	r	x	m	w	g	e	m	n	o	m
n	r	h	k	m	o	n	u	v	n	r	u	s	n	u	m
o	u	o	n	q	a	d	o	p	u	x	d	v	u	o	r
p	q	b	p	h	q	b	h	p	g	p	d	h	b	g	p
q	p	d	g	a	j	g	y	d	q	g	d	j	p	g	y
r	r	n	m	o	v	u	n	r	o	u	r	m	v	t	r
s	x	a	z	v	s	e	z	a	e	x	v	y	x	e	s
t	h	d	f	j	t	l	h	t	f	j	k	l	t	i	f
u	n	u	v	m	r	v	n	m	y	o	u	v	n
v	r	e	y	x	u	y	n	v	r	v	u	y	r	m	x
w	u	m	n	u	w	x	v	w	m	n	a	w	v	u
x	x	z	s	k	v	h	x	u	k	z	r	s	f	h	x
y	p	g	j	u	y	q	j	y	i	p	q	v	y	u	g
z	s	e	z	a	x	a	v	k	z	s	k	x	v	s	e

Small Letters الحروف الصغيرة

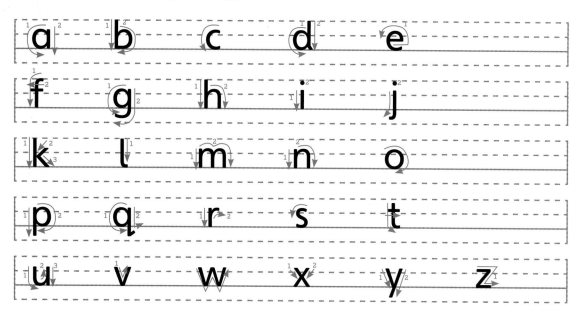

a   b   c   d   e

f   g   h   i   j

k   l   m   n   o

p   q   r   s   t

u   v   w   x   y   z

3 **Write** ٣ اُكتب

Copy the letters a – e. اِنسخ الحروف

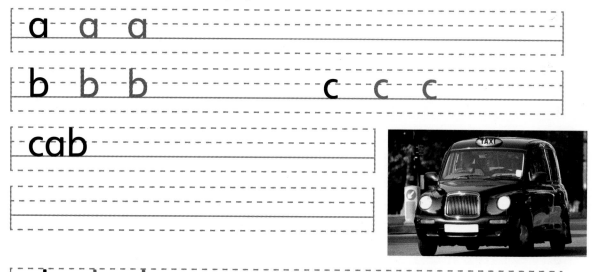

a a a a

b b b   c c c

cab

d d d   e e e

bed

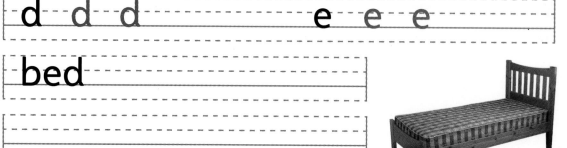

Listen and write. اسمع واكتب

4 Write أُكتب ٤

Copy the letters f – j. اِنسخ الحروف

f f f f   g g g

bag

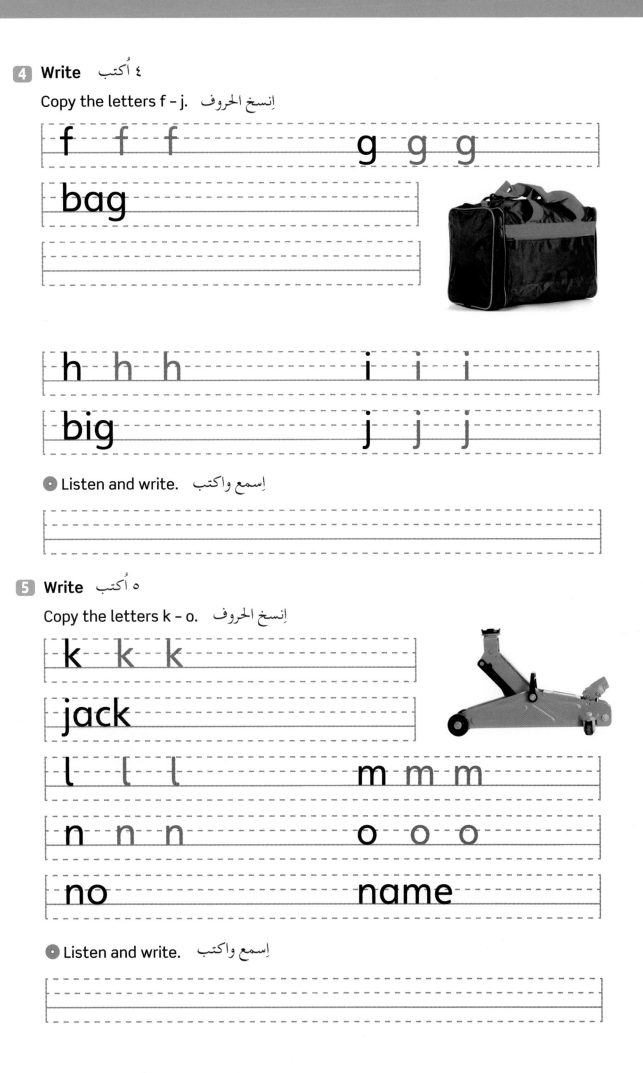

h h h   i i i

big   j j j

● Listen and write. اِسمع واكتب

5 Write أُكتب ٥

Copy the letters k – o. اِنسخ الحروف

k k k

jack

l l l   m m m

n n n   o o o

no   name

● Listen and write. اِسمع واكتب

6 **Write** اُكتب ٦

Copy the letters p – t. اِنسخ الحروف

p p p p   q q q

pen

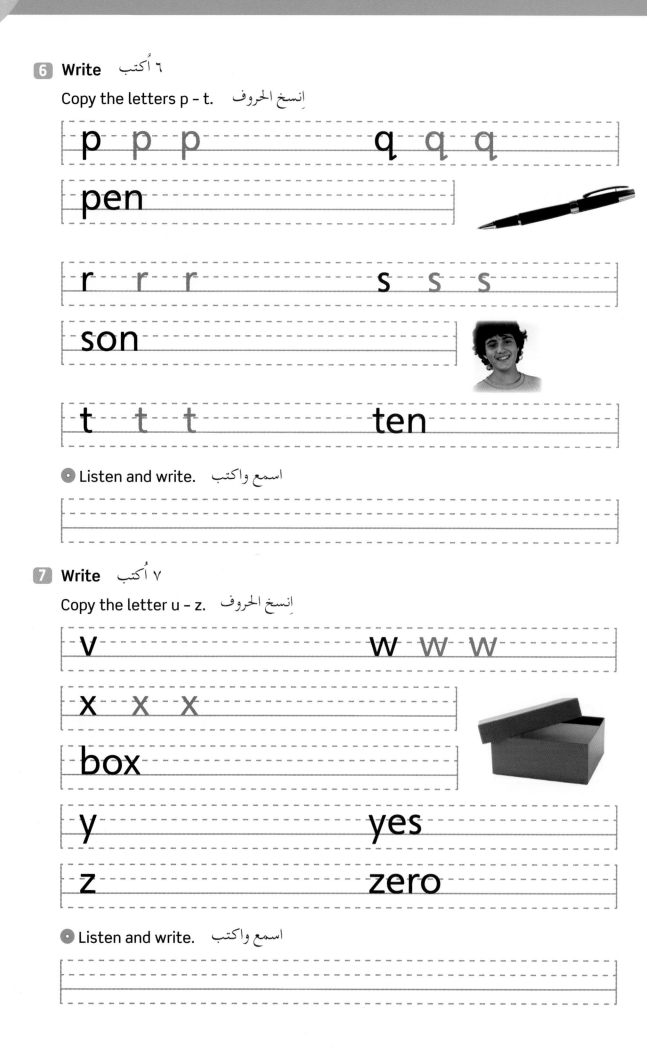

r r r r   s s s

son

t t t t   ten

● Listen and write. اسمع واكتب

7 **Write** اُكتب ٧

Copy the letter u – z. اِنسخ الحروف

v   w w w

x x x

box

y   yes

z   zero

● Listen and write. اسمع واكتب

Counting العد

1 Read ١ اِقرأ

0 zero

1 one   a book   one book

6 six   six keys

2 two   two books

7 seven   seven bags

3 three   three books

8 eight   eight boxes

4 four   four cars

9 nine   nine cars

5 five   five pens

10 ten   ten pens

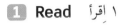

2 🔊 **Listen and circle** ٢ اِسمع وارسم

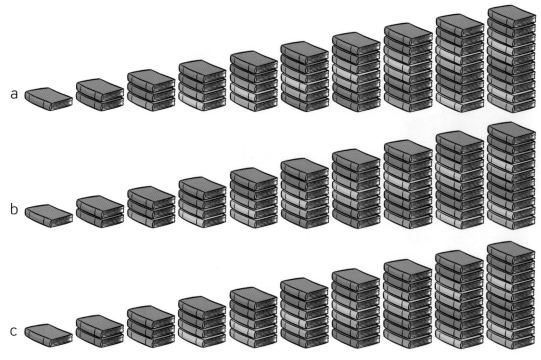

a

b

c

3 **Read and match** ٣ اِقرأ وماثل

six books
two bags
five cars
three boxes
eight keys
four pens
one man
two bees

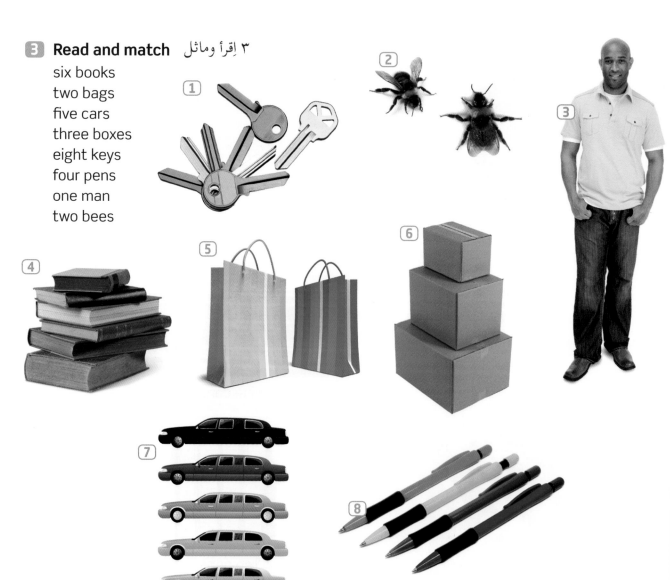

Names الأسماء

1 Read ١ اِقرأ

What's your name?

My name's Bryan.

My name's Carol.

My name's	Tom		My name's	Mary
	John			Jane
	Alexander			Anna
	Paul			Kate
	Ryan			Emma

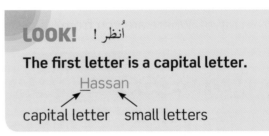

LOOK! اُنظر !

The first letter is a capital letter.

Hassan

capital letter   small letters

2 Write ٢ اُكتب

What's your name? ؟ ما اسمك

My name's James Broadbent.

What's your name?

My name's

Countries البلاد

1 Read ١ اِقرأ

Where are you from?

I'm from England.

I'm from Oman.

LOOK! أُنظر ! الحرف الاول حرف كبير

The first letter is a capital letter.

Oman

capital letter   small letters

2 Write ٢ أُكتب

I'm from Egypt. Where are you from?

Morocco   Spain   Bahrain

France   Algeria   Sudan

Egypt   Tunisia   Oman   Italy

United Arab Emirates (UAE)

India   Scotland   Syria   Japan

Lebanon   Saudi Arabia   England

I'm from

Cities المدن

1 Read ١ اقرأ

Where are you from?

I'm from Cairo.

LOOK! أنظر !

The first is a capital letter.

Cairo

capital letter   small letters

2 Write ٢ أُكتب

Where are you from? I'm from _____

3 Match ٣ ماثل

City

Paris
Athens   Berlin
Tokyo   Cairo
New Delhi
Cardiff
Istanbul
Riyadh   London
Barcelona   Tunis
Rome
Rabat

Country

Tunisia
United Kingdom
Japan
France   Germany
Egypt   Morocco
Spain
Saudi Arabia
Italy   Greece   India
Wales   Turkey

4 Write ٤ أُكتب

Name: ....

City: ....

Country: ....

Telephone number: ....

Punctuation علامات الترقيم

full stop	.	النقطة – علامة الوقف
question mark	?	علامة الاستفهام
comma	,	الفاصلة
apostrophe	'	الفاصلة العليا
exclamation mark	!	علامة التعجب

1 Hello. Hello, Sue!
2 How are you? Fine, thanks.
3 My name's Sue. I'm from England.

exclamation mark   question mark   comma   apostrophe

1 Write ١ اُكتب ! ? ' , .

1 My name's Tom

_____

2 I'm from France

_____

3 Where are you from

_____

4 Are you from Jeddah

_____

5 Welcome

_____

6 Can I have tea please

_____

7 Whats the time

_____

8 Its six o'clock

_____

Words الكلمات

2 **Write in the Arabic words** ٢ مائل

Here are 24 English words you already know! هنا ٢٤ كلمة إنجليزية تعرفها من قبل اُكتبها باللغة العربية
Write the Arabic words.

A a aspirin _____		**M m** mechanic _____	
B b battery _____		**N n** nurse _____	
C c camera _____		**O o** offside _____	
D d doctor _____		**P p** passport _____	
E e express _____		**R r** radio _____	
F f film _____		**S s** sandwich _____	
G g goal _____		**T t** taxi _____	
H h Happy Birthday _____		**V v** vase _____	
I i ice-cream _____		**W w** workshop _____	
J j jacket _____		**X x** x-ray _____	
K k karate _____		**Y y** yacht _____	
L l lemonade _____		**Z z** zebra _____	

1 Meeting people

Lesson 1 Hello!

1 🔘 **Listen and write**

Write A,B,C or D.

2 **Ask and answer**

Practise with other students in the class.

Hello, I'm ... Hello ..., I'm ...

How are you? Fine, thanks.

3 Names

Mary Brown	Hello, Mary. Hello, Mrs Brown.	Sue Long	Hello ... _____
Tom Brown	Hello, Tom. Hello, Mr Brown.	John Main	Hello ... _____
Mark James	Hello... Hello...		

4 Say

Choose a name. Practise with a partner.

Latifa Al-Rashid
Jane Clark
Sarah Ward
Selwa Yasser
Mary Brown
Ann Barry

Hello, I'm ...

Saeed Darwish   Mohammed Yousef
Sam Smith   Tom Brown
Gary Kent
John Main

Hello, Mr/Mrs ..., I'm ...

LOOK!
I'm Tom Brown.
I am Tom Brown.

5 ◉ Listen and write.

Write A,B,C or D

_____ _____ _____ _____

Write under each picture: Hello? Hello! Hello? Hello.

LANGUAGE

Hello/Hi.	Mr ...
I'm ...	Mrs ...
I am ...	
How are you?	Fine thanks.

Lesson 2 My name's Bond

1 ● **Listen and write**

Write A,B,C or D

What's your name, please?
Main, John Main.
M-A-N-E?
No. M-A-I-N.

Hello. Are you Mrs Ward?
Yes.
My name's Nadia.
Oh, hello, Nadia. How are you?

Hello, Mr Darwish?
No. My name's Ilham Ramic.
Oh, I'm sorry.
That's all right.

Hello. My name's Tom Brown.
Hello, Mr Brown. How are you?
I'm fine, thank you.

2 Ask and answer

Practise with other students in the class.

Hello. My name's ... Hello, ... How are you? I'm fine, thank you.

3 ◉ Listen and say

☐ ☐ sorry

☐ ☐ hello

☐ ☐ thank you

☐ ☐ all right

☐ ☐ ☐ How are you?

4 Ask and answer

I'm sorry.

That's all right.

Practise with other students.

Hello. Mr Darwish?   No. My name's ...

Oh, I'm sorry.   That's all right.

LOOK!

My name's ...   = My name is ...

That's all right = That is all right.

5 Read and say

Spell these names. For example:

Main- M-A-I-N.

Kent Brown Sarah Ward Darwish Jones

Rashid Yousef Clark Latifa Barry Smith

LANGUAGE

Are you ...?

What's your name, please?

My name's ...

I'm fine.

I'm sorry.

That's all right.

Thank you.

Lesson 3 This is Ahmed

1 🔊 **Listen and write**

Write A,B, or C.

①

A Ali, this is my friend David.
Hello, Ali.
Hi. How are you?

B Hello, Peter. How are you?
Hello Chris, I'm fine. Chris this is Kate.
How do you do?
Pleased to meet you.

C Hello, Ahmed. How are you?
Oh, not bad thanks. James, this is Saleem Saeedi.
How do you do, Mr Saeedi?
Pleased to meet you.

2 🔊 **Listen and say**

☐ ☐ ☐ ☐   ☐   ☐ ☐ ☐
How do you do?   Pleased to meet you.

3 **Ask and answer**

Introduce other students like this:
A: Hello, ...This is ...
B: How do you do?
C: How do you do?/Pleased to meet you.

4 🔊 **Listen and say**

Numbers 0-5:
0-zero   1-one   2-two   3-three   4-four   5-five.

5 🔘 Listen and say

The alphabet:

A B C D E F G H I J K L M N O P Q R S T U V W X Y Z

Listen and say these letters.

| A H J K | B C D E G P T V | Q U W |

| F L M N S X Z | | | R |

6 Read and say

Read these car numbers to a partner.

HUV 513   420 GA 162   PZ 4522 K   2002 JS

BA 1145   KVT 511F   40320 LQX   4015 CR 233

LOOK!

is

My name **is** Tom. (My name**'s** Tom.)
That **is** all right. (That**'s** all right.)
This **is** Ahmed.

LANGUAGE

This is ...
Pleased to meet you.
Not bad.
Friend
first name
family name
numbers 0-5

Lesson 4 Good morning

1 ● **Listen and write**

Write A, B, C or D.

A Good night.
   Good night.

B Good afternoon, ITC.
   Hello. My name's John Main.

C Good morning.
   Good morning.

D Good evening.
   Good evening, Mr Main.
   How are you?
   Fine thanks. And you?
   I'm fine.

2 ● **Listen and say**

☐ ☐   ☐☐ ☐
morning   afternoon
☐   ☐ ☐
night   evening

3 **Write**

Write **afternoon**, **evening**, **morning**, **night** below the picture.

12.00   5.00-6.00   9.00-10.00

_____   _____   _____   _____

4 **Ask and Answer**

Use: morning/afternoon/evening; fine/not bad/I'm fine, thank you to greet other students like this:

Good morning Saleem. How are you?

Fine thanks. And you?

Not bad.

5 🔊 **Listen and say**

numbers 6-10:
6-six   7-seven   8-eight   9-nine   10-ten

6 **Read these signs:**

BSEC

ITC

ARG

DJE   GLS

LANGUAGE	
Good morning	And you?
afternoon	Telephone number
evening	
night	

Now read these telephone numbers:

837-987,   246-193,   504-451,
632-018,   792-650,   437-915.

STUDY

Hello/Hi.
I'm ...
My name's ...
What's your name, please?

This is Ahmed.

How are you?

Fine thanks.
I'm fine, thank you.
Not bad.

I'm sorry.
How do you do?

That's all right.
How do you do?
Pleased to meet you.

Are you ...?

Yes.
No.

Good morning

Good afternoon

Good evening

Good night.

Mr...

Mrs ...

am
I'm fine.   I am fine.
I'm Tom Brown.   I am Tom Brown.
I'm sorry.   I am sorry.
are
Are you Mrs Brown?
How are you?
is
What's your name?   What is your name?
My name's Mohammed Yousef.   My name is Mohammed Yousef.
That's all right.   That is all right.
This is my friend.

NEW WORDS

Learn these words.

yes
no
a name
a friend
morning
afternoon
evening
night
first
a family
a number
a telephone
a flight
a passport

numbers 0-10
zero, one, two, three, four, five, six, seven, eight, nine, ten

Write other new words here.

_____   _____

_____   _____

_____   _____

_____   _____

_____   _____

_____   _____

_____   _____

2 Family and friends

Lesson 1 Who's that?

1 🔘 **Listen**

Write the names.

grandfather _____   sister _____   son _____

2 **Write**

This is Latifa's family. Write in: **sister**, **brother**, **mother**, **father**, **grandmother**, **uncle** and **grandfather**.

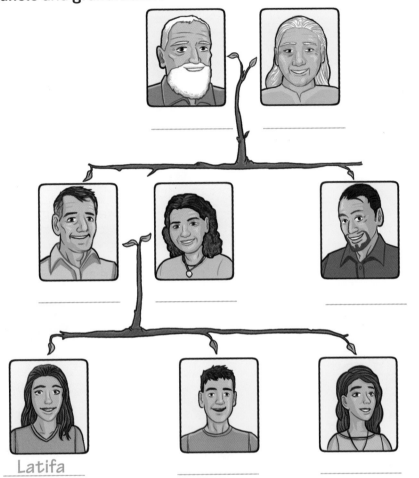

Latifa

LOOK!

my, your, his, her
My name's Latifa.
What's your name?
This is my sister.
What's her name?
This is my son.
What's his name?

3 **Write**

Write **his** or **her**.

a   This is my daughter. What's _____ name?

b   This is my father. _____ name's Mohammad.

c   This is my brother. What's _____ name?

d   This is my grandmother. _____ name's Nora.

e   This is my husband. _____ name's Abdul Karim.

f   And that's my uncle. What's _____ name?

LOOK!

A: That's my
grandfather.
B: He's handsome.
A: This is my
sister, Mariam.
B: She's nice.

LANGUAGE

Who's that?   Who's this?
That is ...   This is ...   I don't know.
What's her name?   Her name's ...   She's nice
What's his name?   His name's ...   He's handsome too.

Lesson 2 Good Luck Hotel

1 🔘 **Listen**

How do you do? I'm Hassan. This is my hotel. It's very good and it's cheap.

This is my son. His name's Seif. He's eight years old.

Yes, I'm eight.

And this is my daughter. Her name's Jamila. She's very young.

How old are you, Jamila?

I'm five and a half.

Write the answers.

a How old is Seif? He's _____ years old.

b How old is Jamila? She's _____ years old.

LOOK!

This is my daughter. **She's** five and a half.
This is my son. **He's** eight.
This is my hotel. **It's** good. **It's** cheap.

2 Write

Write **she's, he's** or **it's**.

a
_____ old.

b
_____ tall.

c
five and a half.

d
_____ small.

e
_____ big.

3 **Match**

Match the adjectives with opposite meanings.

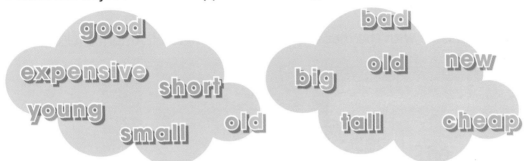

good
expensive
short
young
small
old

bad
old
new
big
tall
cheap

4 **Ask and answer**

Is it ...?   No. It's ...

Is she ...?

Is he ...?

Example: Is it old? No, it's new.

a   tall?   b   good?   c   new?   d   cheap?

5 **Listen and say**

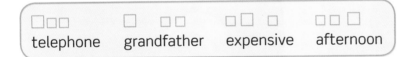

□□□   □   □□   □□ □   □□ □

telephone   grandfather   expensive   afternoon

6 **Listen and say**

Numbers 11-15:   ½ – **a half**

11 – **eleven**   5½ – **five and a half**

12 – **twelve**   12½ – **twelve and a half**

13 – **thirteen**

14 – **fourteen**

15 – **fifteen**

Lesson 3 Where are you from?

1 Match

Match these countries with the maps: Oman, Egypt, England, America (USA).

_____ _____ _____ _____

2 ● Listen

Write in the name of the country.

A Where are you from, Hassan?
I'm from Tanta.
Where's that?
It's in _____.

B What's your name please?
Brown, Mary Brown.
And where are you from, Mrs Brown?
I'm from _____.

C Are you from _____, Sam?
Yes, I am. I'm from the _____.
From New York?
New York? No! I'm from Dallas. That's
in Texas.

D Are you from Kuwait, Leila?
No, I'm not. I'm from Sur.
Sur? Where's that?
It's in _____.

3 ● **Listen and say**

☐ ☐ ☐ ☐   ☐ ☐ ☐☐
Where are you from?   I'm from England.

4 **Ask and answer**

Choose a city and a country from the list. Ask three students:

Where are you from?   I'm from ...   Oran/Algeria
Where's that?   It's in ...   Sousse/Tunisia
Al Hufuf/Saudi Arabia
Latakia/Syria

5 **Ask and answer**

Practise with another student.

☐   ☐ ☐ ☐   ☐ ☐ ☐
Where's   Hassan from?   He's from ...
Mary   She's from ...
Sam
Latifa

LOOK!

I am	from Oman.	(I'm ...)
You are	from England.	(You're ...)
He is	from Egypt.	(He's ...)
She is	from Oman.	(She's ...)
It is	in Oman.	(It's ...)

IMMIGRATION

Where are you from?

6 **Write**

Write **am**, **are** or **is** in the spaces.

A: Where _____ you from?

B: I _____ from Latakia.

A: Where _____ that?

B: It _____ in Syria.

A: And where _____ your friend from?

B: She _____ from Aleppo. That _____ in Syria, too.

LANGUAGE

Where are you from?   I'm from ...
Where's that?   It's in ...
Are you from ...?
Where's ... from?   He's from ...
She's from ...

Lesson 4 Welcome!

1 ⊙ Listen

Officer:	What's your name please?
Tom:	Tom Brown.
Officer:	How do you spell that?
Tom:	B-R-O-W-N, Brown.
Officer:	Where are you from?
Tom:	I'm from England.
Officer:	Are you from London?
Tom:	No, I'm not. I'm from Manchester.
Officer:	Welcome to Jordan, Mr Brown.

2 Write

Complete the immigration form.

IMMIGRATION FORM

NAME: _____

CITY: _____

COUNTRY: _____

PASSPORT NO: FH29431706

3 Read

TOILETS   **IMMIGRATION**

TAXI   **AIRPORT**   **POLICE**   **EXCHANGE**

PUSH   **EXIT**   **PULL**   **CUSTOMS**

Match the sign with the picture.

4 🔘 **Listen and say**

> Numbers 16-20:
> 16 – **sixteen**   17 – **seventeen**   18 – **eighteen**   19 – **nineteen**   20 – **twenty**

5 🔘 **Listen and say**

> These words all have the **p** sound:
> **push, pull, please, spell, passport, expensive, police.**

6 **A game**
Who are you?
Are you from ...? Yes, I am.
Are you ...? No, I'm not.

STUDY

I am …	(I'm)	I'm	eighteen.
You are …	(You're)	You're	from Cairo.
He is …	(He's)	He's	handsome.
She is …	(She's)	She's	very young.
It is …	(It's)	It's	in Yemen.

Are you Mrs Brown?   Yes, I am.
Are you from London?   No, I'm not.

Is he tall?
He is short.

Is she very old?
She's young.

Is it new?
It's old.

Who

Who's this?   Who's that?

What
What's your name?

Where
Where are you from?
Where's that?

How

How are you?	Fine thanks.
How do you do?	Pleased to meet you.
How do you spell that?	B-R-O-W-N
How old are you?	I'm 29.

my, your, his, her
My name's Bond, James Bond.
What's **your** telephone number?
This is Adam and this is **his** son.
Her name's Kiku. She's from Japan.

too
Adam's from Scotland. Oonah's from Scotland **too**.

NEW WORDS

Learn these words.

family	countries	adjectives	numbers 11-20
mother	Algeria	big	eleven
father	Egypt	small	twelve
sister	England	tall	thirteen
brother	Jordan	short	fourteen
grandfather	Kuwait	good	fifteen
son	Oman	bad	sixteen
daughter	Tunisia	nice	seventeen
wife	Saudi Arabia	handsome	eighteen
husband	Syria	young	nineteen
aunt	The United States	old	twenty
uncle	of America (USA)	new	
cousin		cheap	a half
		expensive	

Write other new words here.

_____   _____
_____   _____
_____   _____
_____   _____
_____   _____
_____   _____
_____   _____
_____   _____
_____   _____
_____   _____
_____   _____
_____   _____
_____   _____
_____   _____
_____   _____
_____   _____

Revision A

Grammar

1 **Write**

I am ...	(I'm)
You are ...	(You're)
He is ...	(He's)
She is ...	(She's)
It is ...	(It's)

Write **I**, **you**, **he**, **she** or **it** in the spaces.

a

a Hello, _____'m Mohammad Yousef.

b How are _____?

a _____'m fine thanks.

b

a This is my daughter, Nadia.

b How old is _____?

a _____'s twelve.

c

a Are _____ Julia Williams?

b No, _____'m not.

a Oh, _____'m sorry.

d

a This is my friend, Abed.

b Where's _____ from?

a _____'s from Doha.

b Where's that?

a _____'s in Qatar.

e

a This is my car.

b Is _____ new?

a No. _____'s old.

2 Write

> **Questions**
>
> I am ...   Am I ...?   Are you from London?
> You are ...   Are you ...?   Is he young?
> He is ...   Is he ...?   Is this your son?
> She is ...   Is she ...?
>
> **Question words**
> What ...?   How ...?   How old ...?
> Where ...?   Who ...?

Write the questions.

a _____? My name's Clare Smith.

b _____? C-L-A-R-E S-M-I-T-H

c _____? I'm 19.

d _____? From America.

e _____? No, I'm not from New York. I'm from Dallas.

f _____? That's my father.

g _____? Paul Smith.

3 Write

> I am from Yemen. **My** name's Abed.
> You are from Kuwait. **Your** name's Jaber.
> He is from Egypt. **His** name's Gamal.
> She is from Lebanon. **Her** name's Nabila.

Write **my**, **your**, **his** or **her** in the spaces.

a This is my aunt. _____ name's Fatima.

c Are you Selwa?

No. _____ name's Nada.

b Who's that?

That's my cousin. _____ name's Bashir.

d Is that _____ brother?

No. That's my cousin.

4 Write

> Who's this?   This is ...
> Who's that?   That's ...
>   It's ...

_____ is my sister, Adele.

Write **this** or **that** in the spaces.

Who's _____?

5 Match

Match the questions and answers.

a How are you?

b Are you from London?

c What's her name?

d Is it new?

e How old is Lara?

f Where's London?

1 No. It's old.

2 She's eighteen.

3 It's in England.

4 Habiba.

5 Not bad.

6 Yes, I am.

New Words

6 **The family**

Write these words in the lists:
aunt, mother, uncle, wife, father, brother, daughter, grandfather, sister, husband

son _____

_____

_____

_____

_____

cousin _____

_____

_____

grandmother _____

_____

_____

cousin _____

7 **Numbers 0–20**

Write in the answers.

a eight + nine = _____

b fourteen – _____ = one

c _____ + nine = twenty

d six + thirteen = _____

e _____ + three = fifteen

f sixteen – fourteen = _____

g _____ – eleven = seven

h _____ – four = sixteen

8 **Countries**

Match the countries with the flags.
Saudi Arabia, Italy, Oman, Turkey, Germany, Spain, Egypt, USA

_____ _____ _____ _____

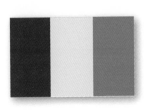  

_____ _____ _____ _____

9 **Write**

Write the answers.

a   Is it good?   No. It's bad.
b   Is it cheap?   No. _____
c   Is Gary old?   No. _____
d   Is your car old?   No. _____
e   Is her house big?   No. _____
f   Is Mona tall?   No. _____

Punctuation

10 **Write**

Write in sentences with punctuation (' , . ?) and capital letters.

a   how are you   _____
b   my names saleem saeedi   _____
c   im from damascus in syria _____
d   its expensive   _____
e   wheres mr brown from   _____
f   are you from riyadh   _____
g   how old is jamila   _____

Spelling

11 **Look**

Find eight mistakes in these sentences.

a   My naime's Ali. I'm fram Saudi Arabia.

b   This is my daghter, Samira. She's twalve years old.

c   My frend is from Oxford. That's in Englend.

d   This is my hotel. It's viry good and cheep.

Read and write

12 Read

This is Simon Star. He's twenty-six years old and he's a famous basketball player. He's very rich too! Simon is from Los Angeles in the United States. His wife is also from the United States, but she isn't from Los Angeles. She's from Miami. Her name's Suzy. They are in Cairo for a basketball game.

Now write.

Name: ....

City: ....

Country: ....

Name: ....

City: ....

Country: ....

13 Read

Read these sentences:

This is my friend, Heba. She's from Cairo in Egypt.
This is my uncle, Waleed. He's from Zarqa in Jordan.

Now write sentences with these words:

a   cousin – Nazir – Muscat – Oman

_____

b   teacher – Mr Walker – Manchester – England

_____

c   aunt – Sabiha – Aleppo – Syria

_____

d   friend – Saleem Hashemi – Dammam – Saudi Arabia

_____

49

● Story: Hello London 1

Ali and his grandfather are in Dubai airport.

1 What's your name please?

Ali Hassan.

2 Window or aisle?

Aisle please.

3 Your passport, please.

4 Flight 3026 to London ...

That's my flight.

5

7 Are you from Dubai?

Yes, that's right.

3 Jobs and Nationalities

Lesson 1 He's a mechanic

1 **Match**

a teacher   a doctor   a student   a nurse   a mechanic

 **a**   **b**    **c**    **d**    **e**

_____   _____   _____   _____   _____

2 ● **Listen and match**

1 ☐

2 ☐

3 ☐

4 ☐

A   This is my friend, Hamid.
Hello, Hamid.
Hello.
He's a mechanic.
Oh! I'm very pleased to meet you!

B   Jamila! Look! I'm a spaceman!
No, you're not, Mohsin. You're just a boy.

C   That's my cousin.
What's his name?
Salem.
Is he a teacher?
No, he isn't. He's a student.

D   Hello. How are you?
Not bad, thanks. Are you a nurse?
No, I'm not. I'm a doctor. My name's Salwa.

Write in the jobs.

a   Salwa is _____ _____

b   Salem is _____ _____

c   Hamid is _____ _____

LOOK!

I'm a spaceman.
She's a doctor.
He's a mechanic.
He's a student.

3 ● **Listen and say**

☐ ☐ a teacher   ☐ ☐ a student   ☐ ☐ a doctor   ☐ ☐ a driver

☐ ☐ ☐ a mechanic   ☐ ☐ ☐ a policeman   ☐ a nurse

Listen again   a tea**ch**er   a me**ch**anic

4 **What's your job?**

I'm ...   a teacher.

a nurse.

a student.

a mechanic.

a policeman.

a doctor.

①

☐

③

I'm _____   I'm _____   I'm _____

④

⑤

⑥

I'm _____   I'm _____   I'm _____

5 **Ask and answer**

Practise with other students in the class.

What's your job?   I'm a ...

I don't have a job.

LOOK!

not (n't)

She's a doctor.   She is not (is**n't**) a nurse.

LANGUAGE

a	**not**
a student	I'm **not** a nurse.
a teacher	You're **not** (You are**n't**) a spaceman.
a mechanic	He's **not** (He is**n't**) a mechanic.
a doctor	
I'm a student.	What's your job?
You're a teacher.	I'm a ...
He's a mechanic.	I don't have a job.
She's a doctor.	

Lesson 2 These are my brothers

1 ● **Listen**

Hello.

This is my uncle, Nasser. He's a pilot.

And these are my brothers, Waleed and Bashir.

How do you do?

They're students at the Capital School.

Are you learning English?

I'm sorry. I don't understand.

They're beginners.

Write.

a Nasser is _____ _____.

b Waleed and Bashir are _____.

LOOK!

they

He's a student.   **They're** students.
She's a student.   **They are** students.

and

These are my brothers Waleed **and** Bashir.

2 Write

Complete the lists.

a doctor   _____

_____   mechanics

a driver   _____

_____   teachers

He's a pilot.   They're pilots.
She's a nurse.   They're nurses.

> **LOOK!**
>
> a student   students
> a pilot   pilots
> a friend   friends

3 ◉ Listen and say

> | sssss | students, pilots, mechanics, mosques |
> | --- | --- |
> | zzzzz | teachers, girls, boys, drivers |
> | iz | nurses, boxes, pages |

> **LOOK!**
>
> This is my friend.
> These are my friends.

4 Ask and answer

Introduce two other students like this.

A: These are my friends, ... and ...
B: Hello. How do you do?
C and D: Pleased to meet you.

5 ◉ Listen and say

> Say these words:
> these, please, meet, evening, three, zero,
> me, cheap, police, nineteen, he, she
>
> Say these words:
> this, six, in, is, big, it, sister, his, beginner, city

6 Write

Write **these, they, is, this, my,** in the spaces.

Latifa: Hello, Sarah.
Sarah: Hello.

Latifa: _____ my sister, Suad.
Sarah: How do you do?
           How do you do?

Latifa: And _____ are _____
           friends, Nora and Fawzia.

Nora and
Fawzia: Hello.

Latifa: _____'re students.

> **LANGUAGE**
>
> This is my brother. **These are** my brothers.
> This is my sister. **These are** my sisters.
> He's a student. **They're** students.
> She's a nurse. **They're** nurses.
> I don't understand.
> **and** – Waleed **and** Bashir

Lesson 3 Are you English?

1 ● **Listen**

Listen to the receptionist and Bob and Ann. They are in a hotel.

R: Where are you from, please?

Bob: We're from England.

R: And your nationality? Are you English?

Ann: That's right. English or British.

R: Are you from London?

Ann: No, we're not.

Bob: I'm from Oxford.

R: Where's that?

Bob: It's near London. And my wife's from Leeds.

R: Leeds. How do you spell that?

Ann: L-E-E-D-S

Put a tick (✓) or a cross (✗)

a Bob and Ann are English. ☐

b They are from London. ☐

c Ann is from Oxford. ☐

d Oxford is near London. ☐

e Bob is from Oxford. ☐

2 **Write**

where, near, right, Egyptian, from, are

a Where _____ you from?

We're _____ Tanta.

b Tanta? _____'s that?

It's _____ Cairo.

c Are you _____?

Yes, that's _____ .

3 ● Listen and say

Practise with other students in the class.

☐ ☐ ☐ ☐   ☐ ☐ ☐   ☐ ☐ ☐
Jordanian   Lebanese   Kuwaiti

-an	-ese	-i
Italian	Sudanese	Bahraini
Moroccan	Japanese	Saudi
Palestinian	Portuguese	Emirati
Syrian	Taiwanese	Iraqi

LOOK!

I'm from Amman in Jordan. I'm Jordanian.
We're from Beirut in Lebanon. We're Lebanese.
She's from Fehahil in Kuwait. She's Kuwaiti.

4 Match

Match the country to the nationality.

Country	Nationality
a The United Kingdom	1 French
b Japan	2 German
c France	3 Dutch
d Holland	4 American
e Germany	5 British
f The United States	6 Japanese

LOOK!

You

Are you Egyptian?   Yes, I am.

Are you Egyptian?   Yes we are.

5 Ask and answer

Who am I?

Are you a man?	Yes, I am.
Are you Syrian?	No, I'm not.
Are you American?	Yes, I am.
Are you a singer?	No, I'm not.
Are you a politician?	Yes, I am.
Are you Barak Obama?	Yes, I am.

Choose: **a singer**, **a politician**, **an actor**

6 ● Listen and say

Numbers 20–30
20–**twenty**   26–**twenty-six**
21–**twenty-one**   27–**twenty-seven**
22–**twenty-two**   28–**twenty-eight**
23–**twenty-three**   29–**twenty-nine**
24–**twenty-four**   30–**thirty**
25–**twenty-five**

LANGUAGE

We are English.
We are from England.
Are **you** English?
Are **you** English?
near
How old are you?
I'm twenty-two **years old**.

numbers 21–30
nationality
country
Yes, **I am**.
Yes, **we are**.

Lesson 4 Where are we?

1 **Match**

> hungry, hot, tired, cold, thirsty

2 **Listen**

3 **Match**

Match the questions and the answers.

a   Where are Sarah and Reem?   1   Yes, she is.
b   Are they tired?   2   They're on a bus.
c   Is Reem hungry?   3   It's near Amman.
d   Where is the bus?   4   Yes, they are.

LOOK!

Questions

We are near Amman.   Are we near Amman?

Where are we?

They are tired.   Are they tired?

LOOK!

not (n't)

We're hungry.   We're **not** hungry.
We aren't hungry.

They're tired.   They're **not** tired.
They aren't tired.

4 Write

Write about these people.

a  _He's happy._

b  _____

c   _____

d  _____

e  _____

f  _____

5 ● Listen and say

we're, near,
they're, where

6 Ask and answer

Are you thirsty?
tired?
cold?
hungry?

Have a ...

jacket   seat   sandwich   drink

Yes, I am.

Thanks.

7 ● Listen

Write A, B, C or D.

_____   _____   _____   _____

Really? Really! Really! Really.

LANGUAGE

an – **an** orange	**Are they ...?**	I think ...
Are we ...?	**They're not ...**	So am I.
We're not ...	**They aren't ...**	Really?
We aren't ...		

STUDY

The verb: to be

I

I am (I'm)

I'm from Lebanon.
I'm Lebanese.
I'm not Jordanian.

Are you Lebanese?   Yes, I am.
Are you Jordanian?   No, I'm not.

You

You are (You're)

You're from England.
You're English.
You're not (You aren't) French.

Am I late?   Yes, you are.
                    No, you aren't. (No, you're not.)

He/She

He/She is (He's/She's)

He's/She's from Saudi Arabia.
He's/She's Saudi.
He's/She's not (He/She isn't) Kuwaiti.

Is he/she Saudi? Yes, he/she is.
Is he/she Kuwaiti? No, he/she isn't.

It

It is (It's)

It's near London.

We

We are (We're)

We're from Egypt.
We're Egyptian.
We're not (We aren't) Tunisian.

Are we late?   Yes, we are.
                    No, we aren't.

They

They are (They're)

They're from Morocco.
They're Moroccan.
They're not (They aren't) Algerian.

Are they Moroccan?   Yes, they are.
Are they Algerian?   No, they aren't.

a

I'm a doctor.   He's a student.   They're nurses.

Have a sandwich/an orange.   Thanks.

What's your job?   I'm a clerk.
What's your nationality?   I'm Lebanese.

don't

I don't have a job.   I don't know.
I don't understand.   I don't speak English.

I think.   I know.   Really?
I'm hungry. **So am I.**

This is my brother.   He's **a** student.
These are my brothers.   They're students.
How old are you? I'm twenty-three **years old.**

NEW WORDS

Learn these words.

jobs

a mechanic
a nurse
a doctor
a student
a teacher
a spaceman
a driver
a policeman
a basketball
  player
a politician
an actor

nationalities

Algerian
American
Bahraini
British
Dutch
Egyptian
English
Emirati
French
German
Iraqi
Italian

Japanese
Jordanian
Kuwaiti
Libyan
Moroccan
Omani
Palestinian
Qatari
Saudi
Sudanese
Syrian
Tunisian
Yemeni

people

a man
a woman
a boy
a girl

things

a sandwich
a seat
an orange

adjectives

hot
cold
hungry
thirsty
tired

countries

Bahrain
France
Germany
Holland
Iraq
Japan
Lebanon

Morocco
Qatar
Sudan
The United Arab
Emirates
The United
Kingdom
Yemen

numbers 21-30

twenty-one
twenty-two
twenty-three
twenty-four
twenty-five
twenty-six
twenty-seven

twenty-eight
twenty-nine
thirty

Write other new words here.

_____   _____

_____   _____

_____   _____

_____   _____

4 In the City

Lesson 1 What's that?

1 Read

Gary and Nour are in a taxi.

> What's that, Nour?

> It's the royal palace.

> Oh. It's beautiful.

> Yes, it is. It's very old.

> And what's that?

> What?

> That new building, there? What is it?

> Sorry, I don't know.

> It's a bank. The Gulf Bank.

> Really? It's very big.

Write the words: **new, big, old.**

a The Royal Palace is very _____.

b The bank is _____.

c The bank is very _____.

> **LOOK!**
>
> What's that? It's **a** bank.
>
> It's **the** Royal Palace.
>
> It's **the** Sheraton Hotel.

2 Ask and answer

What's that? It's the ...
　　　　　　(I don't know.)
Where is it? It's in ...

ⓐ ⓑ ⓒ ⓓ

3 **Write**

Write **that, don't, a, what, there, the** in the spaces.

A: What's that?

B: It's ＿＿＿＿＿＿ Hilton Hotel.

A: And ＿＿＿＿＿＿'s that, ＿＿＿＿＿＿?

C: It's ＿＿＿＿＿＿ bank.

A: And that old building?

B: Sorry, I ＿＿＿＿＿＿ know.

C: ＿＿＿＿＿＿ a hospital.

4 **Write**

Write **a,** or **an** in the spaces.

＿＿＿＿＿＿ building   ＿＿＿＿＿＿ ice cream,

＿＿＿＿＿＿ new school   ＿＿＿＿＿＿ jacket,

＿＿＿＿＿＿ car   ＿＿＿＿＿＿ expensive watch,

＿＿＿＿＿＿ umbrella   ＿＿＿＿＿＿ orange.

> **LOOK!**
>
> It's a watch. It's **an** orange.
> It's a car.
> It's a new car.
> It's **an** expensive car.
>
> We write **an** before **a, e, i, o, u.**

Match the pictures to the words above.

 a
 b
 c
 d

e
 f
g
h

5 **Listen and say**

> where, they're, there, we're, near, here

Listen

A: Look!

B: Where?

A: There.

B: Oh, yes. They're beautiful.

Listen

A: We're here.

B: Near the school?

A: No. Near the hotel.

B: That's good. We're tired.

> **LANGUAGE**
>
> It's a bank.   It's **a** beautiful bank.   It's a house. It's **the** royal palace.
> It's **the** Bank of Bahrain.   It's a hotel.   **an** expensive car
> It's a bank. It's beautiful.   It's **the** Sheraton Hotel.   there, here

Lesson 2 Is it far?

1 ⊙ **Listen and write A or B in the boxes**

Excuse me, where's the KPM building?
Pardon?
The KPM building?
It's there, look.
Oh yes. Thanks.

Excuse me, where's the Capital English School?
It's near the bank.
Is it far?
No, not far. It's about half a kilometre.

LOOK!

next to   near
            not far from

2 **Ask and answer**

A Where's   the market?
             the Habib Bank?
             the hospital?
             the police station?
             the Good Luck Hotel?

B It's near the airport.
             the school.
             the mosque.
             the Royal Palace.
             the Kuwaiti Building.

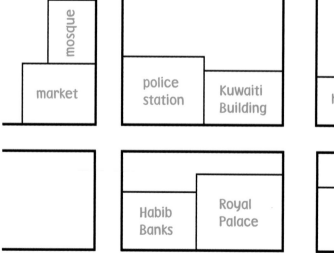
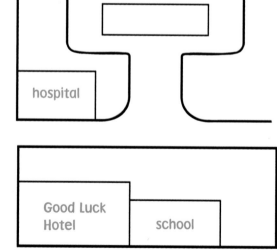

3 **Write**

Write **airport, the, pardon, about, next, far, excuse, where, not** in the spaces.

A: _____ me, _____'s

the airport?

B: _____?

A: Where's the _____?

B: It's _____ to _____

hospital.

A: Is it _____?

B: _____ far. It's _____

one kilometre.

4 ● **Listen and say**

☐   ☐ ◨ ☐
Where's the bus station?

◨ ☐ ◩
Is it far?

☐   ☐ ◨
What's your name?

☐ ☐ ☐ ◩ ☐
Are you from London?

☐ ◨ ☐ ☐
How old are you?

☐ ☐ ☐ ◩ ☐
Are they American?

5 ● **Listen and say**

Numbers 30 – 69:

30 – **thirty**	31 – **thirty-one**	32 – **thirty-two**
40 – **forty**	41 – **forty-one**	42 – **forty-two**
50 – **fifty**	51 – **fifty-one**	52 – **fifty-two**
60 – **sixty**	61 – **sixty-one**	62 – **sixty-two**

6 ● **Listen**

Circle the number you hear.

30 31 (32) 33 34 35 36 37 38 39

40 41 42 43 44 45 46 47 48 49

50 51 52 53 54 55 56 57 58 59

60 61 62 63 64 65 66 67 68 69

LANGUAGE

next to
not far from
Is it far?
Where's the...?
Excuse me.
Pardon?

4

Lesson 3 The market

1 🔵 **Listen**

Sarah: What are those, please?
Khalifa: They're dates. Have one.
Sarah: Thanks. They're sweet.
How much are they?
Khalifa: Two pounds for a kilo.
Sarah: Er ... half a kilo, please.
And are these lemons?
Khalifa: Yes, that's right. They're
one pound for one kilo.
Sarah: OK. One kilo, please.

Find the answer.

Sarah pays
a one pound
b two pounds
c three pounds
d one pound fifty

for the dates and lemons.

2 **Match**

a banana, a watermelon, an apple, an orange, a lemon, a date.

a

b

c

_____ _____ _____

d

e

f

_____ _____ _____

3 **Ask and answer**

A
What's this?
What are these?

B
It's a lemon.
They're dates.

4 Ask and answer

How much is this radio?
How much are these dates?

It's 50 pounds.
They're one rial a kilo.

LOOK!

dirham, dollar, pound, rial, dinar
a kilo
They're five rials a kilo.
(They're five rials for one kilo.)

5 Write

Write **much, sweet, these, they, expensive, are ('re), very, pounds** in the spaces.

A: What are _____?

B: They _____ apricots.

A: Are _____ nice?

B: Yes, they're _____ nice

and _____ .

A: How _____ are they?

B: 20 _____ a kilo.

A: They're _____!

6 ● Listen and say

A: What are those?
B: These?
A: No. Not those. Those!
B: Ah. Those. I don't know.
those, know, no, old, cold, don't

LANGUAGE

What are these? These apples are ... How much is ...?
What are those? Those dates are ... How much are ...?

4

Lesson 4 Streets and roads

GREEN STREET

1 Read and match

a. Excuse me. Is this the road to the airport?

Yes, it is.

b. What's the problem?

It's the clutch.

c. Super or normal?

Super, please. Full.

d. Is this White Street?

No, it's Green Street.

1

2

3

4

2 Match

Write the words under the pictures.

a garage, a lorry, a street, a bus station, a road, a bus, a petrol station

b

c

d

e

_____   _____   _____

f

g

_____

LOOK!

American English	British English
gas	petrol
truck	lorry
cab	taxi

3 Write

Write the words in the dialogue:
much, **next**, **mosque**, **where**, **dinars**, **please**, **it**

A: Taxi!

B: Yes?

A: Momtaz Hotel, _____ .

B: _____ 's that?

A: _____ 's in King Street. _____ to the _____ .

B: Yes, I know.

A: How _____ is it?

B: Two _____

A: All right.

4 Ask and answer

A	B
Taxi!	Yes.
Africa Street, please.	Where's that?
Near the park.	I know.
How much is it?	10 pounds.
All right.	

Ask for:
Beirut Street – near the bus station
The Palace Hotel – near the airport
The Habib Bank – near the hospital
Tunis Street – near the royal palace

5 ● Listen and say

Numbers 70-100:
70–**seventy**   71–**seventy-one**   72–**seventy-two**
80–**eighty**   81–**eighty-one**   82–**eighty-two**
90–**ninety**   91–**ninety-one**   92–**ninety-two**
100–**a hundred**

6 ● Listen and say

sh	sta**ti**on, na**ti**onality, Engli**sh**, **Sh**eraton.
tsh	mu**ch**, wat**ch**, **ch**eap, clut**ch**, sandwi**ch**

LANGUAGE

What's the problem?   It's ...
Is this ...?   Yes, it is.
                       No, it isn't.

Is this the road to ...?
I know.

STUDY

It's **a** bank.

It's **the** HSBC bank.

It's **a** house.

It's **the** airport.

---

an – before **a**, **e**, **i**, **o**, **u**
an apple, **an e**xpensive car, **an i**ce-cream, **an o**range, **an u**mbrella

---

It's a beautiful building.	They're beautiful buildings.
It's a sweet orange.	They're sweet oranges.

there

here

next to

not far from

---

this, that, these, those

What's **this**?	It's a lemon.
What'**re these**?	They're lemons.
What's **that**?	It's a date.
What'**re those**?	They're dates.

How much

How much is it? How much are they?

What's the problem?
Is this the road to ...? Yes, it is. No, it isn't.

NEW WORDS

Learn these words.

places	in the city	shopping	adjectives
a building	a road	a watermelon	sweet
a royal palace	a street	an apricot	fresh
a school	a lorry (truck)	dates	full
a hospital	a taxi (cab)	a banana	empty
a hotel	a bicycle	a lemon	
a bank	brakes	a kilo	**numbers**
a house	clutch		thirty
a market	a kilometre		forty
an airport			fifty
a park			sixty
a bus station			seventy
a petrol (gas) station			eighty
			ninety
			a hundred.

Write other new words here.

_____   _____
_____   _____
_____   _____
_____   _____
_____   _____
_____   _____
_____   _____
_____   _____
_____   _____
_____   _____
_____   _____
_____   _____
_____   _____
_____   _____
_____   _____

REVISION B

Grammar

1 **Write**

I am ...	It is ...
You are ...	We are ...
He is ...	They are ...
She is ...	

Write **am**, **are** or **is** in the spaces.

Waleed and Bashir _____ students at the Capital English School. They _____ Bahraini. Waleed _____ from Jidhafs, a small town near Manama, and Bashir _____ from Muharraq. The school _____ in Manama.

My name _____ Khalifa Yayha. I _____ from Sfax in Tunisia. My wife's name _____ Afifa. She _____ also from Sfax. We _____ Tunisian. I _____ an officer in the army and my wife _____ a teacher.

2 **Answer**

Am I ...?	Yes, you are.	No, you aren't.
Are you ...?	Yes, I am.	No, I'm not.
Is he ...?	Yes, he is.	No, he isn't.
Is she ...?	Yes, she is.	No, she isn't.
Is it ...?	Yes, it is.	No, it isn't.
Are we ...?	Yes, we are.	No, we aren't.
Are they ...?	Yes, they are.	No, they aren't.

Answer these questions.

a   Are your friends from Sudan? No, _____ . They're Egyptian.

b   Is Omar Kuwaiti? No, _____. He's Bahraini.

c   Are Samia and Fawzia from Tunisia? Yes, _____ .

d   Is Selwa Egyptian? No, _____ . _____ Palestinian.

e   Are you Moroccan? No, _____ . _____ Algerian.

f   Is Eman Omani? Yes, _____ .

g Are Waleed and Bashir from Syria? No, _____ . _____

   from Bahrain.

h Is Sarah Lebanese? Yes, _____ .

i Is Zainah Yemeni? No, _____ . _____ from Saudi Arabia,

Now answer this question.

j Are you English? No, _____ . _____ .

3 Write

> It's **a** bank. It's **the** Bank of Bahrain.
> It's **a** hotel. It's **the** Good Luck Hotel.
> Where's **the** market? Where's **the** airport?
> She's **a** teacher. He's **a** teacher. They're teachers.
> **an** apple, **an** English book, **an** ice-cream, **an** orange, **an** umbrella.

Write a, an, the or (-).

a Where's _____ Capital English School, please? It's near _____

   airport.

b Is he _____ singer? No, he's _____ actor.

c It's _____ beautiful car. Yes, but it's _____ expensive car too!

d What's that? It's _____ watermelon. It's very sweet. And what are those?

   They're _____ apricots.

e What's that building, there? Is it _____ bank? No. It's _____ hotel.

   It's _____ Palace Hotel. It's _____ new.

4 Write

> It's a building. It's tall.   They're dates. They're sweet.
> It's a tall building.   They're sweet dates.
> The building is tall.   The dates are sweet.

Change the sentences.

a It's a big watermelon.   The watermelon _____ big.

b They're expensive cameras.   The _____ .

c They're old men.   The _____ .

d It's a beautiful park.   The _____ .

e It's a new house.   The _____ .

f They're nice sandwiches.   The _____ .

5 **Write**

Write **this**, **that**, **these** or **those** in the spaces.

New words

6 **Nationalities**

Write in the nationalities.

Country	nationality	Country	nationality
Algeria	_____	Saudi Arabia	_____
Bahrain	_____	Sudan	_____
Egypt	_____	Syria	_____
Iraq	_____	Tunisia	_____
Jordan	_____	The United Arab Emirates	_____
Kuwait	_____	Yemen	_____
Lebanon	_____	France	_____
Libya	_____	Germany	_____
Morocco	_____	Holland	_____
Oman	_____	Japan	_____
Palestine	_____	The United Kingdom	_____
Qatar	_____	The United States	_____

7 Places

What are these places in the city? Write: **airport, hotel, park, road, bank, house, market, bus station, school, mosque, petrol station.**

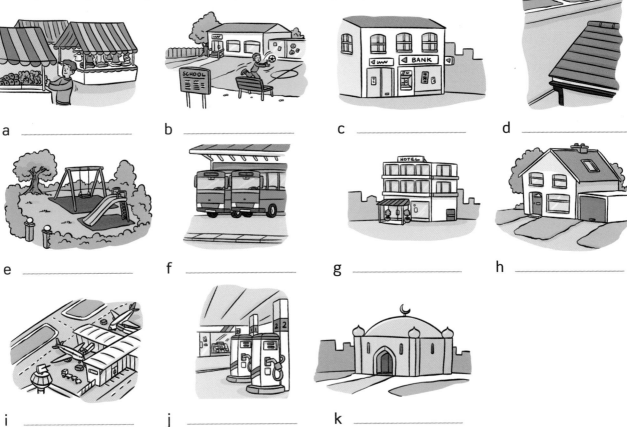

a _____

b _____

c _____

d _____

e _____

f _____

g _____

h _____

i _____

j _____

k _____

8 Jobs

What are these jobs? Write: **teacher, driver, student, mechanic, policeman, secretary, doctor, nurse, pilot, singer, actor, politician, spaceman**

a _____

b _____

c _____

d _____

e _____

f _____

g _____

h _____

i _____

j _____

k _____

l _____

m _____

Punctuation

9 **Write**

Write these sentences with punctuation (' , . ?) and capital letters.

a   theyre lebanese _____

b   wheres the bank of egypt _____

c   its not far from the gulf hotel _____

d   is this green street _____

e   whatre those _____

f   im not french im german _____

Spelling

10 **Look**

Find 17 spelling mistakes.

My naime's Aziza Jassim and I'm a studant at teh Gulf English Scool. I'm from Dubai in the Unitd Arab Emirates.

My husbend is a driaver. He issn't from Dubai. He's fram Sharjah.

My hose is very smal, but it's viry nice. It's in Cairo Streat. It's naxt to a new mosqe. It's not fur from the aireport.

Read and write

11 **Read**

Read this paragraph and write **but** and **and** in the sentences.

The Palace Hotel is in Garden City in Cairo. It's very near the River Nile _____ it is next to a small park. The hotel is very beautiful, _____ it is not expensive. A room in the hotel is about $30 a night. The hotel manager is Egyptian. His name is Samir Awad _____ he is from Alexandria.

12 **Write**

Join these sentences with **and** or **but**.

a   I am tired. My sister is tired, too.

_____

b   I am from Bahrain. My wife is from Saudi Arabia.

_____

c   The jacket is nice. It's very expensive.

_____

d   My name is Selwa Jassim. I am from Fuyayhil in Kuwait.

_____

e   The new airport is beautiful. It is very far from the city.

_____

f   My cousin is 28 years old. He's a mechanic in a garage.

_____

g   My grandfather is old. He's a good driver.

_____

13 **Write**

Write about this hotel.

Nasser Hotel – small hotel – centre – Amman/Kings Street – near – a mosque/
nice – not expensive/manager – Jordanian/Rashid – from Aqaba

_____

_____

_____

_____

_____

_____

_____

B

● Story: Hello London 2

The next day

At Hyde Park

5 What's it like?

Lesson 1 That's mine!

1 🔘 **Listen**

Dan: Excuse me. That's my suitcase.
Tom: No, it isn't. It's our suitcase.
Dan: Well, where's mine?
Mary: What's it like?
Dan: It's black with a red handle.
Tom: I think that's yours – over there.
Dan: Hey. That's my suitcase!

Find Dan's suitcase.

2 **Ask and answer**

That's my ...   No, it isn't. It's mine!
Is this my ...?   Yes, it's yours.

3 **Write**

Write **like, my, your, yours, mine, that, black** in the spaces.

A: Excuse me. Is this _____ camera?

B: No, it's not _____ .

A: What's your camera _____?

B: _____ camera's small and _____ .

A: Ah. I think this is _____ .

B: Yes. _____'s it. Thank you very much.

> **LOOK!**
>
> That's **my** suitcase.   That's **mine**.
> That's **your** suitcase. That's **yours**.

4 Write

What colour is it?

a <u>It's black.</u>

c _____

b _____

d _____

What colour are they?

a  <u>They're green.</u>

c _____

b  _____

d _____

5 Write

What is it? **It's** a black suitcase.
What are they? **They're** black suitcases.

a <u>It's a black suitcase.</u>

b _____

c  _____

d _____

e _____

f _____

LOOK!

our, their

This is **our** suitcase.

That's **their** suitcase.

LANGUAGE

It's **my** suitcase.
It's **mine**.
It's **your** suitcase.
It's **yours**.
It's **our** suitcase.
It's **their** suitcase.

What's it like?
What colour is it?
What colour are they?

Lesson 2 Whose is this?

1 **Read and match.**

a  Is that his? No. I think it's hers.

b Whose car is this? It's my brother's.

c Is this yours? No, it's theirs.

d Whose is this? It's ours.

2 **Ask and answer**

Whose ... is this? It's ...'s.
Whose ... are these? They're ...'s.

> **LOOK!**
>
> **'s**
> Whose car is this? It's my brother's.
> It's Mark's.
> It's Samia's.

3 Write

Write mine, yours, his, hers, ours, theirs in the spaces.

a   That's Mr and Mrs Brown's room.
    It's _____ .

b   This book is Ahmed's. It's _____ .

c   Look. My name is in the book. It's _____ , not yours!

d   This is our house. It's _____ .

e   That's Mariam's handbag. It's _____ .

f   Have this seat. It's not mine, it's _____ .

LOOK!

That's **my**/**your**/**his**/**her**/**our**/**their** suitcase.
That's **mine**/**yours**/**his**/**hers**/**ours**/**theirs**.
That's **Dan**'s suitcase.
That's **Dan**'s

4 Ask and answer

Is that Latifa's grandfather?

Yes, it is.

Is that Latifa's ...?   Yes, it is.
                         No. I think it's her...

5 Match

passport, visa, ticket, money, suitcase, handbag

a   b   c   d    e   f

_____   _____   _____   _____   _____   _____

6 ● Listen and say

who, who's, whose
blue, two, you, fruit, student, new, suitcase

LANGUAGE

Whose is this?	It's mine.
Whose car is this?	yours.
	his/hers.
	ours/theirs.
	It's Latifa's.

5

Lesson 3 She's got green eyes

1 **Listen**

Selwa and Mary are at the airport. They are with Selwa's brother, Awad.

S: Mariam's very late.

M: It doesn't matter.

S: Yes, but it's ten o'clock.

M: What's your sister like?

A: She's quite tall and thin.

M: Like you.

A: Yes. And she's got black hair and green eyes.

M: Green eyes. Really?

S: Yes, beautiful green eyes.

M: How old is she?

S: She's 22.

A: Look. There she is! Mariam.

2 **Match**

a He's tall and thin.

b She's short and fat.

c They're short and thin.

d They're tall and fat.

> **LOOK!**
>
> has got
> What's she like?
> She**'s got** green eyes.   She **has got** green eyes.
> What's he like?
> He**'s got** black hair.   He **has got** black hair.

①  ②  ③  ④

3 **Match**

①   ②   ③   ④   ⑤

_____ _____ _____ _____ _____

a He's got short, black hair and brown eyes.

b He's got brown hair and blue eyes.

c He's got grey hair and brown eyes. He's got a moustache.

d He's got fair hair and blue eyes.

e He's got a beard and a moustache.

4 Write

Write the words **right, brown, tall, like, short, got, he** in the spaces.

A: What's Simon Star _____?

B: He's _____ big, _____ eyes.

A: And his hair?

B: It's _____ and black.

A: Is _____ tall?

B: Not very _____ - but he's not short.

A: Medium?

B: That's _____ .

LOOK!
quite, very

He's **very** tall.   He's tall.   He's **quite** tall.   He's **not very** tall.   He's short.

5 A game

Who is he? Who is she?
Choose someone in the room.

She's ...	He's ...
She's got ... eyes/hair.	He's got ... eyes/hair.
	a beard.
	a moustache.

6 ◉ Listen and say

Silent letters
The **r** is silent

fair, hair – She's got fair hair.
matter, brother, sister, short

LANGUAGE

What's he like?
What's she like?
She's got ... hair.
He's got ... eyes.
quite / very / not very
It doesn't matter.

What's your father like?

He's tall and he's got grey hair.

Eyes?

Yes, he's got two.

Lesson 4 How many?

1 ● **Listen**

Nour and Gary are having tea
in the company canteen.

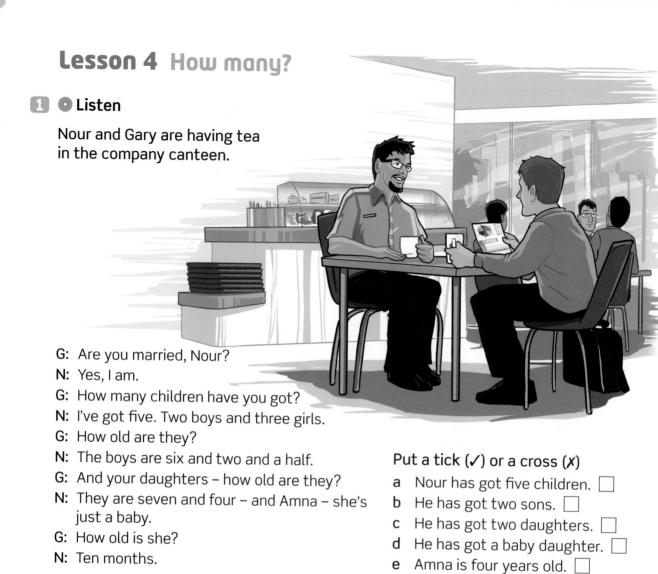

G: Are you married, Nour?

N: Yes, I am.

G: How many children have you got?

N: I've got five. Two boys and three girls.

G: How old are they?

N: The boys are six and two and a half.

G: And your daughters – how old are they?

N: They are seven and four – and Amna – she's
just a baby.

G: How old is she?

N: Ten months.

Put a tick (✓) or a cross (✗)

a   Nour has got five children. ☐

b   He has got two sons. ☐

c   He has got two daughters. ☐

d   He has got a baby daughter. ☐

e   Amna is four years old. ☐

LOOK!

How many children have you got?   **I've** got five

I **have** got five.

child – children

I've got one child.

I've got five children.

---

2 **Ask and answer**

How many ... have you got?

I've got ...

children, girls, boys

brothers, sisters

watches

cameras

radios

English books

cars

keys

I haven't got any ...

3 ◉ **Listen**

Complete the form.

IMMIGRATION FORM

First Name: ....   Family Name: ....

City: ....   Country: ....

Nationality: ....

Married/Single: ....

No. of Children: ....

Address in Jordan: ....

LOOK!

Are you **married**?   Yes, I am.
No, I'm not.   I'm **single**.

4 ◉ **Listen and say**

Numbers 100-200:
100 – a hundred
101 – a hundred and one
110 – a hundred and ten
120 – a hundred and twenty
135 – a hundred and thirty-five
148 – a hundred and forty-eight

153 – a hundred and fifty-three
169 – a hundred and sixty-nine
172 – a hundred and seventy-two
184 – a hundred and eighty-four
198 – a hundred and ninety-eight
200 – two hundred

5 ◉ **Listen and say**

☐ ☐   ☐ ☐   ☐ ☐   ☐☐
children   canteen   married   address
☐☐   ☐ ☐   ☐ ☐   ☐ ☐
baby   moustache   ninety   nineteen

LOOK!

100 – a hundred (or **one** hundred)
101 – a hundred and one
(or **one** hundred and one)
200 – two hundred

6 ◉ **Listen and say**

Plurals
ssss   book**s**, date**s**, jacket**s**, passport**s**
zzzz   son**s**, brother**s**, daughter**s**
iz   hous**es**, watch**es**, box**es**

LANGUAGE

How many ... have you got?   Are you married?
Have you got ...?   Are you single?
I've got ... I have got ...
I haven't got any.

STUDY

Whose is this?
Whose suitcase is this?

It's	my your his her our their	suitcase.	It's	mine. yours. his. hers. ours. theirs.
It's	Latifa's	suitcase.	It's	Latifa's.

What's it like?	It's blue with a red handle.
What's she like?	She's very tall and thin.
What's he like?	He's short and fat.
What colour is it?	It's green.
What colour are they?	They're green.

I've got …	I have got …	I haven't got …
He's got …	He has got …	He hasn't got …
She's got …	She has got …	She hasn't got …
Have you got any children?	Yes. I've got two.	
Has he got …?		
Has she got …?		
How many … have you got?	I've got four. I haven't got any.	

He's got short black hair.

She's got long fair hair.

I'm sorry I'm late.	It doesn't matter.

NEW WORDS

Learn these words.

things
tea
coffee
snacks
fruit juice
a wheel
a handle
a handbag
a suitcase
a ticket
a visa
an address
a pick-up

people
a child
a grandchild
a baby
an officer
the army

adjectives
quite
very
long
short
thin
fat
tall
pretty
married
single

colours
black
blue
brown
green
grey
red
white
yellow
blonde (hair)
fair (hair)

the face
eyes
hair
a beard
a moustache

places
a room
a canteen
a village

numbers 101-200
a hundred and one, a hundred and two, ... two hundred

Write other new words here.

_____   _____

_____   _____

_____   _____

_____   _____

_____   _____

_____   _____

_____   _____

_____   _____

_____   _____

_____   _____

_____

Lesson 1 The second door on the right

1 🔊 Listen

Write A, B or C.

A
Excuse me. Where's Mrs Brown's classroom?
Go along the corridor and it's the third door on the left.
Thanks very much.

B
Where's room 205?
It's on the second floor.
The second floor? Is there a lift?
It's over there, but it's broken.

C
Good morning.
Good morning. Where's Mr Saeedi's office, please?
It's up the stairs.
On the third floor?
Yes. It's the second door on the right.

2 Ask and answer

A
Where's ... office?

B
Go along the corridor.
It's the first   room on the left.
          second   right.
          third

HUDA MOHAMMAD

MOHAMMAD YOUSEF

SALEM SAEEDI

THE MANAGER

MRS BAKER

MR WEST

LOOK!

| Stop | Wait | Go | Go | Wait |

3 ● **Listen and say**

1st – 10th:
1st – **first**   2nd – **second**   3rd – **third**   4th – **fourth**   5th – **fifth**
6th – **sixth**   7th – **seventh**   8th – **eighth**   9th – **ninth**   10th – **tenth**

Numbers 300-1000:
300 – **three hundred**   400 – **four hundred**   500 – **five hundred**
600 – **six hundred**   700 – **seven hundred**   800 – **eight hundred**
900 – **nine hundred**   1000 – **a thousand**

4 **Ask and answer**

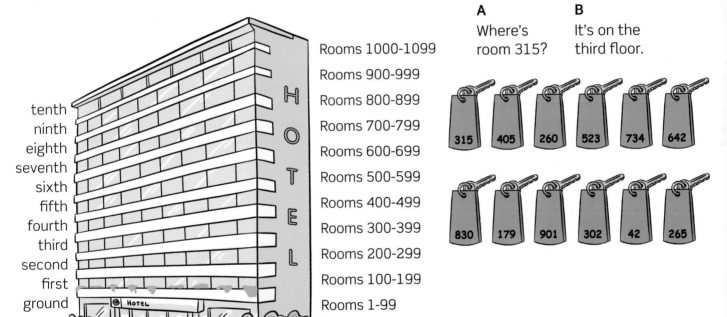

| | A | B |
| | Where's room 315? | It's on the third floor. |

tenth
ninth
eighth
seventh
sixth
fifth
fourth
third
second
first
ground

Rooms 1000-1099
Rooms 900-999
Rooms 800-899
Rooms 700-799
Rooms 600-699
Rooms 500-599
Rooms 400-499
Rooms 300-399
Rooms 200-299
Rooms 100-199
Rooms 1-99

315   405   260   523   734   642
830   179   901   302   42   265

5 ● **Listen and say**

left, red, second, secretary, yes, very,
lift, in, is, this, single, thin, big, women

LANGUAGE

on the left	Go!
on the right	Stop!
on the first floor	Wait!

Is there a ...?
It's broken.
Go along ...

Lesson 2 David's village

1 Read

This is a picture of David's village in England. It's a very small village. On the left there is a shop and next to the shop there's a small restaurant. On the right there's a library and next to it there's a primary school. The village has also got a garage. It's between the school and the restaurant. It's in the middle of the village.

What are they?

a _____

b _____

c _____

d _____

e _____

LOOK!

between

B is **between** A and C

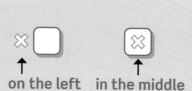

on the left   in the middle   on the right

---

2 Ask and answer

Where's the ... ?	It's	next to ...
Where are the ...?	They're	near ...
		between ... and ...
		on the left.
		on the right.
		in the middle.

a   the library?
b   the shops?
c   the school?
d   the restaurant?
e   the garage?

LOOK!

There is	a mosque.
There are	two shops.

Questions:

There **is** a garage. **Is there** a garage?
There **are** two shops. **Are there** any shops?

3 **Look and say**

There's ...

There are ... between ... and
on the left/right
next to

1 **Student A**. Talk about this street. **Student B**. Look at page 67 of the workbook.

a bank   a restaurant   a hotel   two shops   a garage   a school

2 **Student B**. Look at page 67 of the workbook. **Student A**. Write the names of the buildings.

_____ _____ _____ _____ _____

4 **Write**

Write **are, has, quite, there, a, got, village, primary, is ('s)** in the spaces.

A What's your _____ like Bashir?

B It's _____ nice. It's small.

A Is _____ a school?

B Yes, there _____ a
_____ school.

A Is there _____ mosque?

B Yes. There _____ two.

A And _____ it got a hotel?

B No. But, it's _____ a small
restaurant.

5 **Read**

On the ground floor there's a kitchen, a sitting room,
a small dining room and a toilet. Upstairs there are three bedrooms and a bathroom.

Match the questions and the answers.

a How many bedrooms are there?
b Where's the kitchen?
c Is there a sitting room upstairs?
d Where's the bathroom?
e Is there a dining room on the ground floor?
f Has it got a dining room upstairs?

1 No, it hasn't.
2 It's on the ground floor.
3 It's upstairs.
4 Yes, there is.
5 There are three.
6 No, there isn't.

6 ● **Listen and say**

third, fourth, fifth, sixth,
seventh, eighth, ninth, tenth,
thin, thanks,
there, they're, their,
these, those, this, that, brother,
father, mother

LANGUAGE

There is
There are
Is there (a) ...?
Are there (any) ...?
How many ... are there?

between ... and ...
in the middle
It's got ...
Has it got ...?

Lesson 3 Can I speak to Mrs Roberts?

1 ● **Listen**

Write A, B or C.

A
Hello. 567 2343.
Hello. Is Gary Jones there, please?
I'm sorry, he's not here today.
Oh. I'll phone again tomorrow. Goodbye.
Goodbye.

B
Good morning. ITC.
Good morning. Can I speak to Mrs Roberts, please?
Yes. Who is that?
Salem Darwish.
Just a moment please, Mr Darwish.

C
Good afternoon. Middle East Oil Company.
Can I speak to Sam Smith, please?
I'm sorry. Mr Smith is busy.
Oh can I speak to his secretary?
Certainly.

2 **Ask and answer**

LOOK!

Can I ...
Can I speak to Mr Jones?
Can I have a kilo of oranges?
Can I have a coffee please?

A
Can I speak to ... please?

B
I'm sorry. He's out.
She's busy.
He's not here.
Yes. Just a minute.

a	Mrs Ward	(✓)
b	Ahmed	(✗)
c	The manager	(✗)
d	Mr Saeedi	(✓)
e	Selwa	(✗)
f	Simon Star	(✗)
g	Mr Main's secretary	(✓)

3 Write

Write in these words: **can, minute, sorry, morning, today, speak, wife**

A: Good _____ . Capital English School.

B: Good morning. Can I _____ to Mr Brown please?

A: I'm _____ Mr Brown is not here _____ .

B: _____ I speak to his _____?

A: Yes. Just a _____ please.

LOOK!

I'll phone again tomorrow. = I **will** phone again tomorrow.

4 ⊙ Listen and say

Days of the week
Saturday, Sunday, Monday, Tuesday, Wednesday, Thursday, Friday

What day is it today? _____

What day is it tomorrow? _____

5 How many?

a How many days are there in a week? _____

b How many weeks are there in a year? _____

c How many days are there in this month? _____

d How many months are there in a year? _____

6 ⊙ Listen and say

□□ □	□□□	□ □	□ □
tomorrow	telephone	broken	today

_____ _____ _____ _____

_____ _____ _____ _____

Write these words in the right place:

between, reception, office, sixteen, manager, second, banana, corridor

LANGUAGE

Can I speak to …?
Can I have …?

He's busy.
    out.
    not here.

Just a minute.
I'll phone again …

today, tomorrow
days of the week

Lesson 4 Peter's classroom

1 Read and match

Hello, Peter. Can I help you?

Yes, please Tom. Where's my classroom?

It's on the first floor, the third room on the right.

Thanks very much.

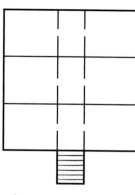

Where's Peter's classroom? Put an X.

LOOK!

Go. Come here. Come on. Sit down.

2 Read

Write these words in the list: **desks, table, books, CD player, cupboard, wall, board, windows, teacher's desk, door.**

This is Peter's classroom. There are 15 desks and chairs in the room. On the left there are two windows. On the right there's a table with a CD player and some books on it. On the wall in the middle, there's a board. Near the board is the teacher's desk. There's a big cupboard near the door.

a _____
b _____
c _____
d _____
e _____
f _____
g _____
h _____
i _____
j _____

LOOK!

in

There are 15 tables in the room.

on

There's a cassette recorder on the table.

3 **Ask and answer**

Where's the ...?   It's ...
Where are the ...?   They're ...
a   the cupboard
b   the desks
c   the board
d   the books
e   the teacher's desk
f   the picture
g   the chairs

LOOK!

Can I help you?   I'll show you.
        speak to Ahmed?   I'll phone tomorrow.
        have a coffee?

4 **Write**

Write **along, door, I'll, far, very, second, help, on, workshop.**

A: Hello. Can I _____ you?

B: Yes. Where's the _____?

A: It's not _____ . _____ show you.

B: Thanks.

A: Go _____ this corridor. The workshop is _____ the right.

B: Is it the first _____?

A: No. That's the toilet. It's the _____ door.

B: Thank you _____ much.

5 ● **Listen and say**

door, or, board, floor, wall, four, fourth
Sounds and spelling
Listen: door, room

6 ● **Listen and say**

Silent letters
cupboard, stairs, first, third

LANGUAGE

Can I help you?   I'll show you.
Come here.   in the room
Come on.   on the table
Sit down.   on the wall

STUDY

There is a mosque.   Is there a garage?
There are two shops.   Are there any shops?

There's a shop **between** the garage **and** the restaurant.
There's a garage **on the right**.
There's a hotel **on the left**.
There's a school **in the middle of** the village.

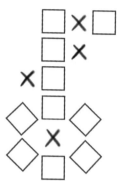

There are 15 tables **in** the room.
There's a CD player **on** the table.

Can I ...?
Can I speak to Mrs Roberts, please?

She's busy.
        not here.
        out.
Yes.   Just a minute.

Can I have a kilo of oranges, please? Certainly.
Can I have a coffee, please?

Can I help you?

I'll phone again tomorrow.   I'll ... = I will ...
I'll show you.

Go! Stop! Wait! Come! Sit!

Go along the corridor. Go up the stairs. Go down the stairs.
Come on. Come here. Sit down.

Prepositions
up   down   along   on   in   between

NEW WORDS

Learn these words.

rooms
a kitchen
a bathroom
a sitting room
an office
a toilet
a bedroom
a classroom
a photocopying room
a computer room
a workshop

things
a table
a door
a window
a picture
a chair
a wall
a desk

places
the stairs
a lift
a restaurant
a coffee shop

time
today
tomorrow
day
week
month
Saturday
Sunday
Monday
Tuesday
Wednesday
Thursday
Friday

adjectives
broken
busy
large

verbs
to go
to stop
to wait
to speak
to help
to have
to show
to phone
to come

numbers
first, second, third, fourth, fifth, sixth, seventh, eighth, ninth, tenth.
one hundred, two hundred, … a thousand

Write other new words here.

_____   _____
_____   _____
_____   _____
_____   _____
_____   _____
_____   _____
_____   _____
_____   _____
_____   _____
_____   _____
_____   _____
_____   _____
_____   _____
_____   _____

REVISION C
Grammar

1 **Write**

That's my book.	That's mine.
your	yours.
his	his.
her	hers.
our	ours.
their	theirs.

Write **my, your, his, her, our, their** in the spaces.

Stop! That's _____ camera!

This is _____ ice-cream.

That's _____ car.

This is _____ seat, sir.

That's _____ pick up.

This is _____ book.

2 **Write**

Write the sentences like this:

<u>That's mine.</u>

_____

_____

_____

_____

_____

3 **Write**

I have got ...	Have I got?	It has got ...	Has it got ...?
You have got ...	Have you got ...?	We have got ...	Have we got ...?
She/He has got ...	Has she/he got ...?	They have got ...	Have they got ...?

Write **have** or **has**.

a   Our village _____ got two schools.

b   _____ you got any children?

c   She _____ got long black hair.

d   _____ the students got their books?

e   I _____ not got any oranges.

4 **Write**

> **There is** a book on the table.
> **There are** two books on the table.

Write **is** or **are**.

In the classroom there _____ two windows on the right. On the left there

_____ a door, and on the wall in the middle there _____ a board. There

_____ a table near the board and there _____ five or six books on it. In

the middle of the classroom there _____ twelve desks and twelve chairs. On

the right, between the windows, there _____ a large cupboard.

Now draw the classroom.

5 Match

> Can I help you?
>   have ...?
>   speak to ..?

Match the sentences with the pictures.

a  (Can I speak to Saeed, please?)

b (Can I help you?)

c (Can I have a kilo of carrots?)

d (Can I have a coffee, please?)

New Words

6 Rooms

Write the names of the rooms:
office, kitchen, classroom, dining room, toilet, sitting room, bedroom, bathroom

a _____ **b** _____ **c** _____ **d** _____

e _____ **f** _____ **g** _____ **h** _____

7 Colours

Write four sentences about colours.
For example: My car is red and white.
Lemons are yellow.

_____

_____

_____

_____

My car Lemons The door	is are	black. white. brown. red. yellow. green. grey. blue.

8 Numbers

Write the other numbers.

first _____ _____

_____ _____

_____ _____

_____ _____

_____ _____

9 Numbers

Write these numbers:

149 _a hundred and forty-nine_ 613 _____

175 _____ 861 _____

284 _____ 999 _____

392 _____ 1000 _____

Punctuation

10 Write

Put in punctuation and capital letters.

a wheres mrs browns classroom _____

b hes got two children _____

c im simon stars secretary _____

d that's latifas _____

e can i speak to john main please _____

f ill phone again on sunday _____

g the managers office is on the left _____

h ive got brown eyes and grey hair _____

Spelling

11 Look

Find 12 spelling mistakes.

My naime's Mona. I'm tharty-two yeers old and I'm from London in England. I'm a teacher in a primary school. I'm maried and I've got tow children, a boy and a gairl. My husbend is a clerk in a bank. Our flat is neer the centre of London. It's got two bedroms, a siting room, a kitchen and a bahtroom. It's on the forth floor.

Read and Write

12 Read

Read about Damascus Street.

I live in a small street in Cairo. It's called Damascus Street. We've got three shops, two hotels, a mosque, a café, and a restaurant in our street. There is also a small garage. The garage is on the left, on the corner. It's called Hassan's garage. Hassan's the owner. Next to the garage is a small hotel, the First Class Hotel. It's cheap, but it's not very nice. After that, there's our house. We are between the hotel and a café. There are always many people at the cafe. It's very busy. Next to the café there's a shop. The owner is Mustapha. He's a friend of mine. On the right of the street there's a restaurant and a hotel – the Momtaz Hotel. It has got a large entrance. Next to the hotel there are two small shops. The first is a bakery and the second has got fruit and vegetables. After that, at the end of the street, there's a big mosque.

Now complete the plan.
Write: **shop, bakery, mosque, Momtaz Hotel, restaurant, First Class Hotel, Hassan's Garage**

13 Write

Write in the missing words

Charles – 30
engineer – oil company – Dubai
married – one son

Charles has _____ blue eyes _____ short fair _____. He's about 30 _____ old. He's got _____ moustache, but he _____ got a beard. He's _____ and quite thin. He's _____ engineer _____ an oil company in Dubai. He's _____ and he's got one son.

Jade – 51
nurse – hospital – London
single

My sister, Jade, has got brown _____ and short grey _____. She's _____ and she's quite slim. _____ 51 years _____. She's _____ nurse in a hospital _____ London. She's not married.

14 Write

Write about these two people:

Jack – 36
taxi driver – London
married – four children

Susan – 43
secretary – ITC – Amman
married – two children

_____   _____

_____   _____

_____   _____

_____   _____

C

⊙ Story: Hello London 3

1. Good morning, Ali. What's the problem?

My grandfather. He's not in the hotel.

2. Not in the hotel? Where is he?

I don't know.

3. Let's look in the street.

OK. Maybe he's there.

4. He's not here.

Look. I'll ask that policeman.

5. Your grandfather? What's he like?

He's small and he's got a grey beard.

6. How old is he?

He's about 65.

Wordlist

A

about	حَوالي
actor	مُمَثِّل
afternoon	بَعْدَ الظُّهر
airline	خَطٌّ جَوِيٌّ
airport	مَطَار
Algeria	الجَزائر (البَلَد)
Algerian	جَزائرِيٌّ
all right	وهُوَ كَذلك
along	عَلَى طُول – بِمُوازاة
America	أمْريكا
American	أمْريكِيٌّ
and	و – لِلإِضافَة
answer	إجابَة – يُجيب
any	أيُّ
apple	تُفّاحَة
apricot	مشمش
Arab	شَخْصٌ عَرَبي
ask	يَسْأل
aspirin	أسرين
atlas	أطلَس
aunt	عَمَّة أو خَالَة

B

baby	طِفْل رَضِيع
bad	سَيِّئ
bag	شنطة – حَقِيبَة
Bahrain	البَحْرين
Bahraini	بَحْرينِيٌّ
bald	أصْلَع
banana	إصْبع مَوْز
bank	بَنْك – ضَفَّة النَّهْر
basketball player	لَاعِب كُرة السَّلة
bathroom	حَمَّام – حُجْرة
battery	بَطارِيَّة
beard	لِحْيَة – ذَقَن
beautiful	جَميل
bedroom	حُجْرة نَوْم
between	بَيْن – وبَيْن
Bicycle	عَجَلة
big	كَبير
black	أسْوَد
blonde	شَقْراء
blue	أزْرَق
book	كِتاب
box	صُنْدُوق

boy	وَلَد
brakes	فَرامِل
British	بَريطانِيٌّ
broken	مَكْسُور
brother	أخٌ
brown	بُنّيَّ
building	مَبْنى – بِنَايَة
bus	أتوبيس
bus station	مَحَطَّة أتُوبيس
busy	مَشْغُول
bye-bye	وَدَاعًا إلَى اللِّقَاء

C

cab	سَيّارَةُ أُجرة
cable	بَرْقِيَّة
camera	كَاميرا – آلَةُ تَصْوير
can I..?	هَلْ يُمْكِن ... ؟
canteen	مَقْصَف
car	سَيّارة
cassette	كاسيت
cassette recorder	جِهازُ تَسْجيل
chair	كُرْسِيٌّ
cheap	رَخيص
child	طِفْل
children (pl.)	أطْفال
city	مَدينة
classroom	فَصْل (حُجْرة دِراسَة)
clerk	كَاتِب (مُوَظَّف)
clutch	دبرياج (القَابِض)
coffee	بُن – قَهْوَة
coffee shop	مَقْهى – مَحل القهوة
cold	بَارد
come	يَأتِي
come on!	يَتَقَدَّم – يَتَطوَّر
comma	فَاصِلة
company	شَرِكة
computer	كمبيوتر (الحَاسِب الآلي)
corridor	طُرقَة – مَمَر – دهليز
country	بَلَد
cousin	ابن العَمَّ
crossword	كَلِمات مُتقاطِعة
cupboard	دُولاب
customs	عَادات

D

Date	تاريخ / تمر (بلح)
daughter	ابْنة
day	يَوْم

desk	مَكْتَب	forty	أرْبَعُون
dinar	الدينار (عُمْلة)	four	أرْبَعة
dining room	حُجْرة المَائدة	fourteen	أرْبَعة عَشر
diploma	دبْلُوم – شَهادة	fourth	الرابِع
dirham	درْهَم (عُمْلة)	France	فَرَنسا
doctor	طَبيب – دُكتُور	freezer	مُحَمِّد
dollar	دُولار	French	فَرَنسيّ
door	بَاب	fresh	طَازِج
down	أسْفَل	Friday	يَوْم الجُمُعة
dozen	دَسْتة	friend	صَديق
driver	سَائق	from	مِنْ
Dutch	هُولَنْديّ	fruit	فَاكِهة
		full	كَامِل
		full stop	نُقطة – عَلامة وَقْف

E

Egypt	مصْر	**G**	
Egyptian	مصْريّ	gallon	جَالُون
eight	ثَمانَية	garage	جَاراج
eighteen	ثَمانَية عَشر	gas	غَاز
eighty	ثَمانُون	German	ألْمانّ
eleven	إحْدى عَشرة	Germany	ألْمانيا
Emirati	إمَاراتيّ (مُواطِن مِنَ الإمَارات)	girl	بِنْت
empty	فَارِغ	Go!	اذهَب !
engineering	هَنْدَسة	Go along…	يَتَقدَّم – يُرافِق
England	إنْجلْترا	goal	هَدَفْ
English	إنْجليزيّ	good	حَسَن
entrance	مَدْخَل	Good afternoon	تَحيَّة بَعدَ الظُّهر
evening	مَسَاء	Good evening	مَسَاءُ الخَيْر
exchange	يَتَبادْل	Good luck!	حَظًّا سَعيدًا
exclamation mark	عَلامة تَعَجُّبْ	Good morning	صَبَاحُ الخَيْر
Excuse me	أتَسْمَحُ لي (لَوْ سَمَحْت)	Good night	تُصبِح عَلَى خَيْر
expensive	غَال	grandfather	جَدٌّ
express	سَريع	grandmother	جَدَّة
eyes	عُيُون	green	أخضَر
		grey	رَماديّ
		ground	أرْض

F

Fair	جَميل	**H**	
family	عائلة	hair	شَعْر
family name	اسْم العَائلة	handle	يَدٌّ
fat	سَمين	handsome	أنيق
father	أبْ	happy	سَعيد
fifteen	خَمْسة عَشر	Happy Birthday!	عيد ميلاد سَعيدٌ
fifth	الخَامِس	Have a…	لِيكُنْ …
fifty	خَمْسُون	Hello!	أهلاً
film	فيلْم	here	هُنا
fine	جَميل – نَاعِم – حَسَّاس	Hi!	مَرحَبًا
first	أوَّل	Holland	هُولندا
first name	الاسْم الأَوَّل	horn	بُوق
five	خَمْسة	hospital	مُسْتَشفى
floor	أرْضيّة		
form	شَكْل		

hot	حَار	lift	مِصعَد (أسانسير)
hotel	لُوكاندة – فُندُق	listen	يَستَمِع
house	بَيْت	long	طَويل
How are you?	كَيْف حَالك ؟	look	يَنظُر
How do you do?	كيف حَالُك ؟	lorry	لُوري
How many...?	كَم (للعَدد) ؟		
How much...?	كَم (للثَمَن) ؟	**M**	
a hundred	مَائة	man	رَجُل
hungry	جَوْعَان	manager	مُدير
husband	زَوْج	market	سُوُق
		married	مُتَزوِّج
I		match	مُبَارَاة – يُضَاهي – يُمَائل
ice-cream	أيس كريم	mechanic	ميكَانيكيّ
immigration	هِجْرَة	middle	وَسَط
in	في	mine	مِلْكي
in the middle	في المُنتَصَف	ministry	وَزارَة
inch	بُوصَة	Ministry of Foreign Affairs	وَزارَة الخَارجيَّة
Iraq	العِرَاق	Ministry of Labour	وَزارَة العَمَل
Iraqi	عِرَاقيّ	minute	دَقيقَة
		mirror	مِرآة
J		Monday	يَوْم الاثْنين
jack	رَجُل رافعة (كوريك)	month	شَهْر
jacket	جَاكتة	morning	صبَاح
Japan	اليَابَان	Moroccan	مَغْربيٌّ
Japanese	يَابَانيّ	Morocco	المَغرب
jeans	بَنطَلُون جينز	mosque	مَسْجِد
job	وَظيفَة – مَهنَة	mother	أُمٌّ
Jordan	الأرْدُن	moustache	شَارب
Jordanian	أردني	Mr	السَّيّد
just a minute	دَقيقَة لو سَمحْت	Mrs	السَّيّدة
		music	مُوسيقَى
K		my	مِلْكي (ضَمير)
karate	كَاراتيه	My name's...	اسْمي ....
ketchup	الكَاتشاب		
key	مُفتَاح	**N**	
kilo	كيلوجرام	name	الاسْم
kilometre	كيلومتر	nationality	الجِنسيَّة
king	مَلك	near	قَريب
kitchen	المَطبَخ (حُجرَة المَطبَخ)	new	جَديد
Kuwait	الكُوَيت	next to	مُلاصق لـ
Kuwaiti	كُوَيتيٌّ	nice	لَطيف
		night	لَيْل
L		nine	تسعَة
late	مُتَأخِر	Nineteen	تسعَة عَشر
Lebanese	لُبنَانيّ	ninety	تسعُون
Lebanon	لُبنَان	Ninth	التَاسِع
left	شمال	No	لا
lemon	لَيمُون	Not bad	لَيسَ سَيئا
lemonade	شَرَاب الليمُونادة	number	عَدَد
Libya	ليبيَا	nurse	مُمَرِضة
Libyan	لِيبيٌّ		

O

o'clock	السَّاعة
office	مَكْتَب
officer	ضَابط
offside	خَارِج النِّطاق
Oh!	آه
old	قَديم – كَبير في السِّنّ
Oman	عُمَان
Omani	عُمَانيٌّ
on	عَلىَ
on the left	في الشِّمال
on the right	في اليَمين
on the … floor	في الطَّابق …
one	واحِد
orange	بُرْتُقَالة
out	خَارِج
over there	هُنَاك

P

page	صَفْح
palace	قَصْر
Palestinian	فَلَسْطِينيٌّ
park	مُتَنَزَّه – مَوقَف سَيَارات
passport	جَوَاز سَفَر
pen	قَلَم
people	نَاس
petrol	بِنزين
petrol station	مَحطَّة بِنزين
phone	صَوْت
photocopying	مَاكِينة تَصوير
picture	صُوْرَة
please	مِنْ فَضلِك
pleased	مَسرُور
pleased to meet you	مَسرُور لِرُؤيتِك
policeman	رَجل شُرطَة
politician	رَجل سياسي
pretty	جَميل
primary school	مَدرسة ابتدائيَّة
pull	يَجذب
puncture	ثُقب في إطار السَّيَارة
punctuation	عَلامَات التَرقيم
push	يَدْفَع

Q

Qatar	قَطَر
Qatari	قَطَريٌّ
queen	ملكَة
queue	طَابُور
quite	تَماماً

R

radio	رَادُيو
read	يَقرَأ
reception	استقبَال
red	أحَمر
rest	يَستريح
restaurant	مَطعَم
rice	أرز
right	صَوَاب
road	طَريق
room	حُجْرَة
royal palace	القَصْر المَلَكيِّ

S

salad	سَلاطَة
sandwich	سَندْوتش
say	يَقُول
Saturday	يَوْم السَّبْت
Saudi Arabia	السَّعُودية (العَربية)
Saudi	سَعُوديٌّ
school	مَدْرَسَة
seat	مَقْعَد
second	ثَان
secretary	سِكرتير (ة)
seven	سَبعَة
seventeen	سَبعَة عَشر
seventh	السَّابِع
seventy	سَبعُون
shampoo	شَامْبُو
shop	مَحَل – مَتَجر
short	قَصير
single	أعزَب – بِمُفرَده
sister	أُخْت
sitting room	حُجْرَة الجُلُوس
six	سِتَّة
sixteen	سِتَّة عَشر
sixth	السَّادس
sixty	سُتُّون
small	صَغير
So am I	وهَكَذَا أَكُون أَنا
son	ابْن
Sorry	آسف
spaceman	رَجُل فَضَاء
speak	يَتَكَلَّم
spell	يَتَهجَّى
spelling	التَهجِّي
stairs	السَّلالم
station	المَحطَّة
stereo	ستريو
stop	يَتَوقَّف – مَوقَف – مَحطة

street	شَارِع
student	طَالِب
Sudan	السُّودان
Sudanese	سُودانيٌّ
suitcase	شَنطة مَلابِس (حَقيبَة)
sun	الشَّمس
Sunday	الأَحَد
sweet	حَلْوى
Syria	سُوريا
Syrian	سُوريٌّ

T

table	تَرابيزة – منضَدة
taxi	تَاكسي – سَيَّارة أُجرَة
tea	شَاي
teacher	مُعَلِّم – مُدرِّس
telephone	التِّليفُون
telephone number	رَقْم التِّليفُون
ten	عَشَرَة
tenth	العَاشِر
thanks	شُكْرًا
thank you very much	شُكْرًا جَزيلاً
that	ذَاكَ
that's all right	هَذا سَليم
their	ملكيَتَهُم
theirs	خَاص بهم
there	هُناك
There is …	يُوجَد (للمُفرد)
There are …	يُوجَد (للجَمع)
these	هؤُلاء
thin	نَحيف – رَفيع
thing	شَيء
third	الثَالِث
thirsty	عَطْشان
thirteen	ثَلاثَة عَشَر
thirty	ثَلاثُون
this	هَذا
those	هؤُلاء
thousand	ألف
three	ثَلاثَة
Thursday	الخَميس
time	وَقْت
today	اليَوم
toilets	دَورات مياه
tomorrow	غَدًا
too	أَيْضاً
tree	شَجرَة
truck	عَرْبة نَقل (سَيَّارة)
Tuesday	الثُلاثاء
Tunisia	تُونُس
Tunisian	تُونُسيٌّ
twelve	اثنا عَشَر
twenty	عشرُون
two	اثنان

U

umbrella	مظلَّة (شَمسيَّة)
uncle	عَم أو خَال
The United Arab Emirates	دَولة الإمارَات العَربية المُتَحدة
The United Kingdom	المَملكة المُتَحدة
The United States of America	الولايات المُتَحدة الأَمريكية
up	أَعلَى
upstairs	في الطَّابِق العُلويِّ

V

very	جدًّا
video	فِيديو
villa	فِيلا
visa	فِيزا (تَأشيرَة)

W

wait	يَنتَظِر
wall	حَائط
watermelon	بطيخ
Wednesday	الأَرْبَعاء
week	أَسبُوع
What?	مَاذا ؟
What's your name?	مَا اسمُك ؟
What's the time?	مَا السَاعة ؟
Where…?	أَين ؟
Where are you from?	من أَين أَنتَ ؟
white	أَبَيض
Who…?	مَنْ … ؟
Who's that?	مَنْ هَذا ؟
wife	زَوجَة
window	نَافذَة
workshop	وَرشَة
write	يكتُب

X

X-ray	أَشِعة إكس

Y

yacht	يَخْت
Year	سَنَة
yellow	أَصفَر
Yemen	اليَمن
Yemeni	يَمنيٌّ
Yes	نَعَم
young	صَغِير

Z

zebra	حمار وَحشيٌّ
zero	صفر